insight text guide

Alison Tealby

Coraline

Neil Gaiman

insight®

▸ innovative ▸ engaging ▸ evolving

First published in 2024, reprinted 2025.

Insight Publications Pty Ltd
3/350 Charman Road
Cheltenham VIC 3192
Australia
Tel: +61 3 8571 4950
Email: books@insightpublications.com.au

www.insightpublications.com.au

Neil Gaiman's Coraline / Alison Tealby

Alison Tealby asserts the moral right to be identified as the author of this work.

ISBNs:
9781923016187 (print)
9781923016194 (digital)

Cover design by Hayley Sinnatt
Layout by Bec Yule @ Red Chilli Design
Edited by Anica Boulanger-Mashberg
Proofread by Janice Bird

Proudly Printed in Australia by Ligare Book Printers

Insight Publications acknowledges the Traditional Custodians of the Country on which we meet and work, the Boonwurrung People of the Kulin Nation. We pay our respects to their Elders past and present, and extend that respect to all Aboriginal and Torres Strait Islander peoples.

contents

CHARACTER MAP

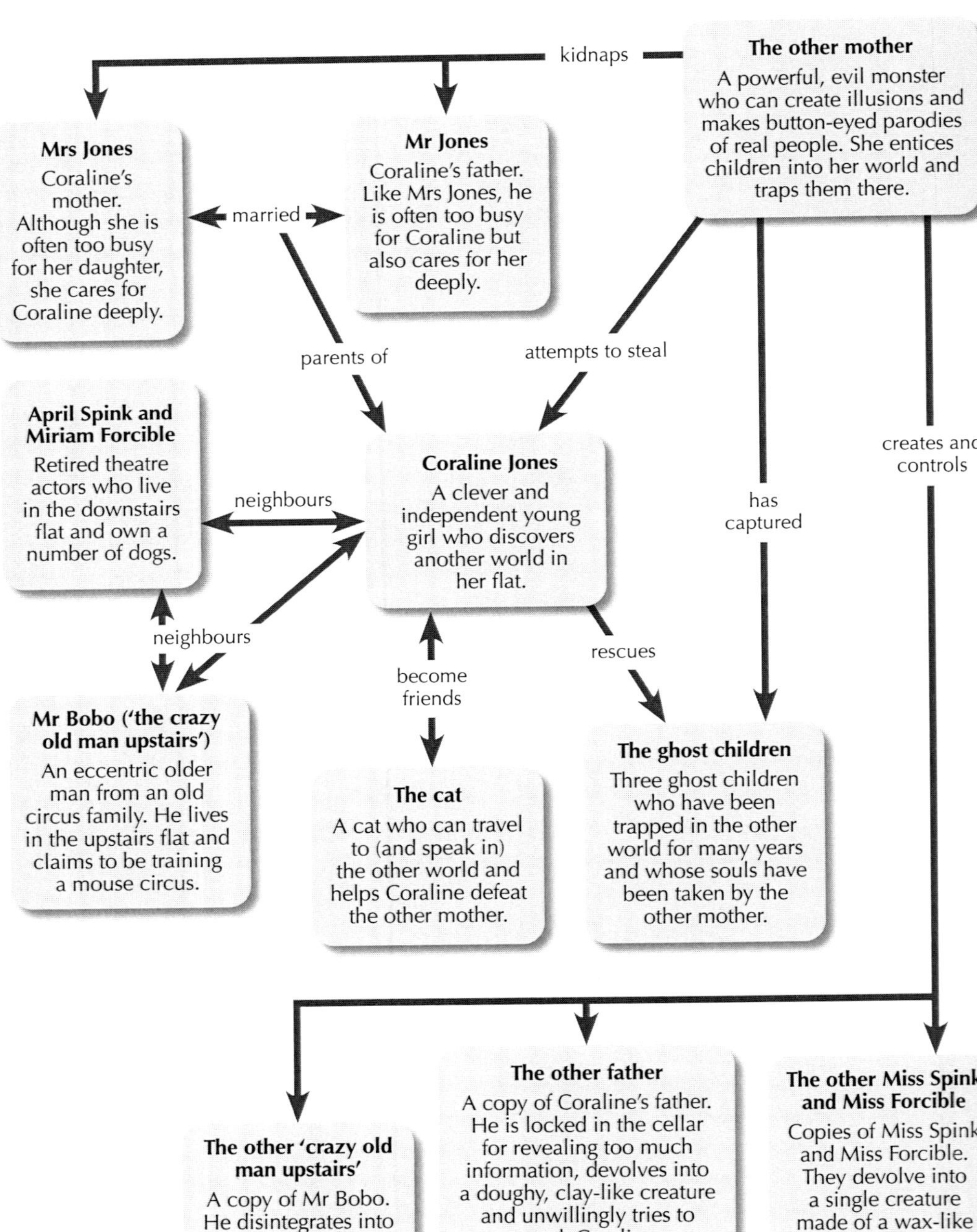

OVERVIEW

About the author

Neil Gaiman is an English author who was born in Hampshire, England, in 1960. His love of books and reading began at an early age. He describes himself as a 'feral child who was raised in libraries' and would spend days reading in a library while his parents were at work (Gaiman 2016, pp.22–3). In 1992, he moved to the United States.

Gaiman began a career as a journalist and published his first book, a biography of the pop band Duran Duran, in 1984, before starting to write graphic novels and long-form fiction. He has since become an acclaimed and prolific author of fiction for children, teens and adults, publishing over forty books and over forty comics. He has also produced works in other mediums, including film and television. Gaiman has a special interest in the genres of fantasy and science fiction, and many of his novels feature magical or fantastical elements.

Gaiman has collaborated with other well-known creatives, including artist Dave McKean and fantasy writer Terry Pratchett, and has topped bestseller lists with various works. Some of his more famous publications include *The Sandman* (1988), *Good Omens* (co-written with Terry Pratchett, 1990), *Neverwhere* (1996), *Stardust* (1999), *American Gods* (2001), *Coraline* (2002) and *The Graveyard Book* (2008). Many of his works have been adapted for film and television, and he has won numerous literary awards including the prestigious Newbery Medal (the highest award for children's fiction in the US) and multiple Hugo Awards (awarded to outstanding science fiction and fantasy works).

Synopsis

Coraline and her parents have recently moved into a large subdivided house that they share with three neighbours: Miss Spink and Miss Forcible, retired theatre actors who live downstairs, and 'the crazy old man upstairs' (e.g. p.14) who claims to be training a mouse circus.

Coraline is on school holidays and frequently bored: the adults don't pay her much attention (the neighbours don't even pronounce her name correctly) and she entertains herself by exploring her surroundings, soon discovering a door in the drawing room that opens to a brick wall. That night, she follows a shadowy creature and finds the door ajar, then returns to bed and dreams of black shapes (likely rats) singing an ominous song. The next day, the old man upstairs passes on a message from his mice, telling her not to go through the door. Miss Spink and Miss Forcible contribute to the mood of foreboding by reading her tea-leaves and telling her that she is in danger, and Miss Spink gives her a stone with a hole in the middle, as a protective charm.

When Coraline unlocks the door, she finds a hallway leading to a flat almost identical to her own, where she meets her 'other mother' and 'other father' (p.39), who appear similar to her parents but have buttons instead of eyes. She explores this strange world and meets the 'other' neighbours, who also have buttons for eyes.

Coraline likes the food and the unusual toys in the parallel version of her flat; however, she is uneasy about the black rats under her bed, which sing an eerie song, and the other old man, who lets them burrow in his clothes. She meets a talking cat that appears identical to a cat she had seen in her own world. The ground-floor flat is now a theatre, where the other Miss Spink and Miss Forcible appear as young women performing to an audience of talking dogs. The other mother and father tell Coraline she can stay with them forever if she lets them replace her eyes with buttons, but Coraline refuses and returns home.

Back in her flat, Coraline can't find her parents, until the cat leads her to a mirror, where her parents appear to be trapped. When Coraline and the cat return to the other world, the other mother denies having anything to do with the disappearance of Coraline's parents and claims they have abandoned her. A rat then brings the other mother the key to the door, allowing her to trap Coraline in the other world. The cat advises Coraline to challenge the other mother because she loves games.

The other father tells Coraline the other mother made everything in this world, and Coraline notices a new snow-globe on the mantelpiece with two people inside, although she does not immediately realise who they are. Outside, the further she walks, the less real the world seems, and when she walks far enough, she ends up back at the house. When Coraline defies the other mother, she locks Coraline behind a mirror to teach her a lesson about manners, claiming it's 'for [her] own good' (p.95).

While locked behind the mirror, Coraline meets three ghost children who explain that the other mother stole their souls. They tell Coraline to flee and ask if she could free their souls. Just before she falls asleep in the tiny, locked room, one of the ghost children tells her to look through the stone – a hint she temporarily forgets. When the other mother lets Coraline out, Coraline suggests a game: if she can find her parents and the souls of the ghost children, the other mother must let them all go. If she fails, Coraline promises to stay and allow the other mother to replace her eyes with buttons. The other mother agrees, swearing by her right hand.

Coraline discovers that looking through the stone allows her to see the souls, and she finds the first in her bedroom, and the second in the theatre downstairs. During this second trip to the theatre, much has changed – the theatre seems abandoned, and there is a sac attached to the wall, within which a nightmarish creature is cocooned; a creature that on closer inspection appears to Coraline to be 'one ghastly object' made up of the other Miss Spink and Miss Forcible (p.120), and that holds in one of its hands the second soul.

The world outside is deteriorating. The other mother gives Coraline a key to the empty flat in the house, where Coraline discovers a monstrous creature, which used to be the other father, in the cellar. It warns her to run, then tries to attack her, as its behaviour is controlled by the other mother. Coraline narrowly escapes, goes to the top flat and faces the other old man, who tries to persuade her to stay. She refuses, and he falls apart into a mass of black rats, one of which holds the third ghost child's soul. The cat decapitates the rat, and Coraline realises she knows where her parents are. With the house disintegrating, Coraline picks up the cat and goes to confront the other mother.

Coraline tricks the other mother into unlocking the drawing-room door then throws the cat at her to distract her, grabbing the snow-globe and escaping to the corridor with the cat. The presence of her parents and the ghost children gives her strength to pull the door closed, though something seems to thump to the floor. Coraline and the cat return home, and Coraline locks the door and falls asleep. When she wakes, she is relieved to find that her parents are back.

Later, Coraline dreams of the ghost children. Although they are happy to be free, they warn her that she is still in danger, then pass on. When she wakes, she sees the other mother's hand searching for the key, which Coraline keeps on a string around her neck. Miss Spink and Miss Forcible read her tea-leaves again, which show a hand-shaped clump. Their dog Hamish has been injured, likely by the hand, and the old man upstairs tells Coraline that something has frightened the mice. The hand reappears at night by Coraline's window.

Coraline goes to an old well she had found when exploring the grounds earlier and lays out a dolls' picnic, with a tablecloth covering the top of the well. She uses the key to lure the hand and tricks it into falling into the well.

Coraline learns that the name of 'the crazy old man' is Mr Bobo, who tells her that the mice consider her their saviour, and he finally learns how to say her name correctly. She returns the stone and falls asleep to the sound of mice playing musical instruments, ready for school the next day.

Character summaries

Coraline Jones

Coraline is a young girl who discovers another world behind a door in her family's flat, where she must rescue her parents and the souls of the ghost children from the dangerous other mother. Coraline is curious, intelligent and independent, and thinks of herself as 'an explorer' (p.24, p.87, p.134).

Mr and Mrs Jones

Coraline's parents don't pay much attention to her when they are distracted by work or chores. However, they care for her deeply. They are trapped in a snow-globe by the other mother and rescued by Coraline.

April Spink and Miriam Forcible

Miss Spink and Miss Forcible are retired actors who live in the ground-floor flat with their dogs. They seem nice, but persistently mispronounce Coraline's name and don't listen to her when her parents go missing. They predict that she is in danger by reading her tea-leaves. Miss Spink gives Coraline the stone with a hole in it, which helps Coraline find the ghost children's souls.

Mr Bobo ('the crazy old man upstairs')

Mr Bobo, who Coraline refers to as 'the old man' or 'the crazy old man' until the final chapter, lives in the upstairs flat. He tells Coraline that he's training a mouse circus and passes on messages from the mice. He also mispronounces Coraline's name; however, he later learns to say it correctly.

The cat

The cat appears to be an ordinary black cat, but it can speak in the other world. It has an arrogant demeanour, and has knowledge of the other mother and her world. It helps Coraline defeat the other mother and they become friends.

The ghost children

The ghost children are three long-dead children who have been trapped by the other mother. Coraline rescues their souls and then sees them in a dream in the real world, where they warn her about the danger she still faces, before passing on.

The other mother

At first, the other mother looks similar to Coraline's real mother, but with black buttons for eyes. She turns out to be an ancient, monstrous figure, also known as 'the beldam', who steals the souls of children. She is responsible for the other world and the people who live in it, and kidnaps Coraline's parents to try to force Coraline to stay with her.

The other father

The other father is a creation of the other mother. He initially resembles Coraline's father but later appears as a monstrous creature who is forced to try to attack Coraline. He is portrayed as not inherently evil but, rather, as under the control of the malicious other mother.

The other Miss Spink and Miss Forcible

The other Miss Spink and Miss Forcible first appear as young versions of their real-world counterparts. They perform in their flat, which resembles a theatre, with a staff and an audience of talking dogs. During Coraline's second visit, the theatre is decrepit and the two women are merged together into a single creature, which holds the second ghost child's soul.

The other 'crazy old man upstairs'

The other old man superficially resembles Mr Bobo; however, he turns out to be made up of numerous black rats. He tries to convince Coraline to stay with the other mother, promising she can have whatever she wants. One of the rats holds the third ghost child's soul.

BACKGROUND & CONTEXT

Context of publication

Gaiman originally wrote *Coraline* for his daughters (to whom he dedicates the book, p.7), and took about ten years to complete it, having begun it in the early 1990s. His daughter Holly, who was around four at the time, enjoyed stories about brave young girls escaping evil witches; after failing to find a scary children's book for her to enjoy, he started writing *Coraline*, initially believing it would be a very short story. However, he soon realised it would be longer and, after becoming busy with other projects, he abandoned it. When he began writing again, Holly was a teenager, so he was motivated to finish the story before his younger daughter, Maddy, also became too old for it (HarperCollins Publishers 2011).

Coraline is often discussed as being very frightening for a children's story, and conversations about this began before publication. Gaiman sent the story to his literary agent, Merrilee Heifetz, who told him it was too scary for children. He suggested she read it to her six- and eight-year-old daughters, Morgan and Emily, to test this. Both girls said that they loved it and that it wasn't too scary, and the book was published. Years later, Morgan told Gaiman that she'd lied – she'd found *Coraline* terrifying, but didn't admit it because she'd wanted to know what would happen next (Gaiman 2016, pp.91–2).

Coraline was well received following publication. It won many awards, including a Hugo Award and a Bram Stoker Award, and earned praise from reviewers and critics. It has been adapted into a graphic novel, a musical and an award-winning animated film, and remains popular with children and adults alike.

Influences on *Coraline*

Gaiman has referenced several influences from his life that inspired aspects of Coraline's story, including the following.

- The house was based on real places: the house where Gaiman lived when he began writing *Coraline,* which, like Coraline's house, had been subdivided into a number of flats; his childhood home's drawing room, which had a door that opened onto a brick wall; and the front room of his grandmother's house, which included oil paintings of fruit, like those in Coraline's drawing room (Gaiman 2013).
- The name 'Coraline' was inspired by a typo that Gaiman made when writing 'Caroline'. Gaiman originally thought he had created the name, but later learned that it was already in use (HarperCollins Publishers 2012).
- Coraline's dislike of 'recipes' was inspired by Gaiman's son Mike who, as a child, disliked Gaiman's more adventurous cooking (HarperCollins Publishers 2012).

Critics and reviewers often suggest that Gaiman was partially inspired by Lewis Carroll's *Alice's Adventures in Wonderland* (1865), noting similarities between the two texts. Gaiman also references the frightening short story 'The New Mother' (1882) by the Victorian children's author Lucy Clifford as a literary inspiration for *Coraline* (Olson 2002).

Gaiman has also described being motivated to write a story for children that was not just frightening, but told its child readers that 'dangerous things can be overcome' (CBC Arts 2009) – a sentiment that is reflected in the adapted quote by GK Chesterton at the beginning of the novel.

Setting

The physical setting of *Coraline* is fairly ambiguous. The reference to London at the beginning of Chapter 3 suggests that Coraline and her family live somewhere in England; however, aside from this, there is little information about the geographical placement of Coraline's house.

Coraline also doesn't make any particular note of social, political or other historical events that would help date the story, and even references to technology are rather vague: Coraline watches television and uses a phone – both popular, relatively enduring technological devices. There are passing references to Mr Bobo collecting a milk bottle and Coraline using a phone book, which hint that the book was written before smartphones became ubiquitous and when milk was commonly delivered to houses in Britain; however, these references are very brief. Although the other Miss Spink and Miss Forcible use a gramophone (an old device that plays recorded music), this could be seen to be part of the strange, circus-like atmosphere of their flat. Consequently, although *Coraline* is set in modern times, the period is indistinct enough that the story could be taking place during any roughly 'contemporary' time.

GENRE, STRUCTURE & LANGUAGE

Genre

Coraline mixes several different genres, including the following.

Children's fantasy and parallel worlds

Coraline is an example of **children's literature** (literature written specifically for children). The focus on Coraline's maturation means it can also be thought of as a **bildungsroman** or coming-of-age story.

Like many of Gaiman's works, *Coraline* can also be considered part of the **fantasy** genre, and it features many fantastical or supernatural elements such as talking animals, a magical new world, creatures that change shape, and a stone with revelatory powers. Similar relevant genres are **fairy tales** and **magical realism**, a type of fiction in which magical elements feature within a realistic setting.

The other world in *Coraline*, accessed through the drawing-room door in Coraline's house, is an example of a **parallel world**. The story of a child entering into a new magical world is also a feature common to other children's fantasy works, including Lewis Carroll's *Alice's Adventures in Wonderland* (1865) and CS Lewis' *The Chronicles of Narnia* series (1950–56).

Coraline is also sometimes called a **dark fantasy**, to account for its more frightening elements. These elements also place it in the tradition of **horror fiction** and the **Gothic** genre.

The Gothic

Coraline can be considered to belong to the tradition of Gothic literature – a genre that began in the 1700s and is known for featuring frightening, creepy or disturbing elements. It includes well-known novels such as Mary Shelley's *Frankenstein* (1818) and Bram Stoker's *Dracula* (1897).

Gothic literature is often defined by the presence of particular **tropes** (elements that recur within a particular genre). Elements in *Coraline* that could be considered Gothic tropes include:

- a large old house with a mysterious, locked door
- foreboding omens, such as the tea-leaves
- a heroine struggling against a powerful evil villain
- ghosts
- spooky and frightening imagery, such as the eerie singing rats; the unnerving tunnel between worlds; the monstrous 'other' characters; the deteriorating other world; and the animated, severed hand.

Coraline also features elements of the **uncanny**. The uncanny refers to something being both familiar and strange, evoking a sense of unease. One way this occurs in *Coraline* is through the parallels between the real and the other world, including the other mother and the people she created, who appear familiar but have significant, disturbing differences that reveal them to be 'a ghastly parody' (p.137). Such parodies or doubles of people can also be called **doppelgangers**.

Gothic texts often use fantastical elements to represent real-world anxieties. Coraline's journey and her struggle against the other mother reflect anxieties about growing up and parent–child relationships.

Fairy tales

Although fairy tales often feature magical elements, they differ from the fantasy genre through their link to traditional folk stories, and they often have a purpose of conveying a moral or message to the reader. The stories of Hans Christian Andersen are well-known examples.

Gaiman positions *Coraline* in the tradition of fairy tales through the epigraph paraphrased from the author GK Chesterton:

> Fairy tales are more than true: not because they tell us that dragons exist, but because they tell us that dragons can be beaten. (p.9)

By choosing this epigraph, Gaiman indicates that *Coraline* is a fairy tale in which the 'dragon' will be beaten, and that demonstrating that 'dragons can be beaten' is at least one of the intentions of *Coraline*.

Other elements in *Coraline* link the novel to the tradition of fairy tales, and to fairies specifically.

- The story's lack of specific details relating to time and place is a feature associated with fairy tales, which often only provide a broad context.
- The other mother, as an evil maternal figure, is an archetypal character frequently seen in fairy tales, such as the evil stepmothers in *Snow White and the Seven Dwarfs* and *Cinderella*. Her magical powers also connect her to the archetype of witches, which are also prevalent in fairy tales. The word 'beldam', which the ghost children use for her, is a very old term that has been used to refer to old women, crones, hags and witches.
- There are also associations between the other mother and legends relating to fairies. These include her desire to kidnap children; her ability to manipulate through illusion; her attempt to trap Coraline by giving her nice food; her love of games and challenges; and the fact that she is bound by her word (she swears on her right hand, and then loses it after she lies to Coraline).
- The stone with a hole in it resembles a hag stone – a stone with a naturally occurring hole. Hag stones have strong ties to folklore, and are often attributed with magical properties such as the ability to bring good fortune, protect from harm, and allow users to see into the fairy realm or see through the illusions of witches or fairies. Miss Spink says the stone is 'good for bad things, sometimes' (pp.30–1) and the cat refers to the stone as 'protection' (p.49). It helps Coraline locate the souls, clear her head and repel the other mother.
- There is a fairy ring made of toadstools near the house (p.13).
- In Coraline's dream, the third ghost child has fairy-like characteristics: she has large butterfly wings and eats flowers (p.164).

Structure

Coraline is a short book (sometimes called a **novella**). The story follows Coraline's journey chronologically, and takes place over a short period of time during her school holidays.

One notable point about the novel's structure is the recurrence of certain aspects of Coraline's real world, which reappear, changed, during her first visit to the other world, and then appear changed again during her second visit. For example, consider the following comparison of Coraline's downstairs neighbours.

Real world	First visit to the other world	Second visit to the other world
Miss Spink and Miss Forcible are elderly retired theatre actors with pet dogs.	The other Miss Spink and Miss Forcible appear as exciting theatre performers with a staff and audience of talking dogs.	The other Miss Spink and Miss Forcible appear misshapen in a cocoon, in a 'derelict' theatre with 'dog-bats' (pp.117–18).

The changes between the real world and Coraline's first visit to the other world shows how the other mother attempts to 'improve' upon Coraline's world, while the changes during Coraline's second visit emphasise the true, frightening nature of the other world.

Coraline's reactions to certain elements repeated at each of these stages also change as she gains greater understanding of her situation. For example:

Real world	First visit to the other world	Second visit to the other world
Coraline is annoyed at her mother for refusing to purchase clothes she likes.	Coraline likes her wardrobe in the other world.	Coraline changes into her dressing gown rather than wear the other world's clothes.

These different responses reveal Coraline's changing attitude to her real world and the other world.

There are also several other aspects of the novel that change notably between the earlier and later chapters.

Earlier chapters	Later chapters
The neighbours call Coraline 'Caroline', and she calls Mr Bobo 'the crazy old man upstairs' (e.g. p.25).	Mr Bobo learns Coraline's name soon after she learns his.
Coraline complains about her father's recipes and is unhappy that her parents ignore her.	Coraline (mostly) eats the recipes and feels appreciative of her parents.
Coraline doesn't believe the mouse circus exists.	Coraline falls asleep to the sound of the mouse circus playing musical instruments.

The repetition of elements, and the way in which they change, conveys important information regarding plot and character development.

Finally, Coraline's journey follows a common storytelling pattern in which a protagonist leaves home, goes on a dangerous adventure, then returns home, having experienced internal change following their ordeal. One of the best-known models to describe such stories is 'the hero's journey', proposed by writer Joseph Campbell. Details of Campbell's theory have been criticised by scholars for various reasons; however, the model can be useful in considering how Coraline's emotional growth relates to the structure of the novel overall.

Language

Coraline also uses language and literary techniques in a variety of other ways to develop the story and create particular effects.

Narrative voice

The story is told in a third-person limited narrative voice. This means that, although the narration is from the point of view of someone outside the story, the narrator stays close to Coraline's perspective, focusing on her experiences. Despite this, the prose style of *Coraline* often does not provide much detail about Coraline's emotions. Critic Richard Gooding suggests this indicates Coraline 'either does not understand or cannot confront her feelings', and readers instead need to infer her emotions through other narrative details, such as her physical responses (Gooding 2008).

Language and character

The different styles of language used in dialogue help to develop characterisation.

- Coraline speaks in a fairly simple, straightforward manner, reflective of her age and personality.
- The cat makes sarcastic, dry remarks and speaks in an aloof manner.
- The other mother speaks in a maternal fashion, calling Coraline 'darling' (p.73, p.77, p.92) and mimicking the kinds of things that parents are expected to say; however, there are also sinister aspects to some of her dialogue, such as when she tells Coraline that she put her own mother in the grave (p.109).
- The ghost children use old-fashioned terms and make outdated references, indicating the great length of time they've been trapped with the other mother. They also sometimes speak in a slightly repetitive, poetic manner: 'A husk you'll be, a wisp you'll be' (p.102).
- Miss Spink and Miss Forcible make many references to famous theatre plays and characters. This is a form of intertextuality and emphasises their feeling of connection to their past as actors. Their other world counterparts also directly quote Shakespeare plays during their performance, emphasising the link between the two pairs.
- Mr Bobo has an excited, repetitious way of speaking that may reflect his origins, as he comes from an old circus family. His style of dialogue contrasts noticeably with that of the other old man, who speaks more calmly – for example, consider the contrast between 'Hey! Hi! You! Caroline!' (p.174) and 'Hello Coraline' (p.43).

→

- The rats sing three menacing songs in unison over the course of the novel, each of which has four lines. Their simple rhyming format makes them feel almost like children's rhymes, except the lyrics are disturbing and threatening. They contribute an element of horror to the novel.

Symbols and motifs

There are several **symbols** (items or elements that represent an idea) and **motifs** (elements that are repeated to highlight a particular idea) in *Coraline* that suggest particular themes or aspects of character.

- The button eyes symbolise the other mother's control.
- Spiders and spiders' webs represent the other mother's spider-like predatory and deceptive nature.
- The mirror in the corridor emphasises the idea of the other world as a strange kind of reflection of the real world.
- The mist suggests confusion and the feeling of being lost.
- Coraline's changing relationship with clothes and food represents her growing independence and changing attitude to the other world.
- Names are significant in terms of the novel's theme of identity. (For more on this, see the discussion of identity in 'Themes, ideas & values'.)

Foreshadowing

Examples of foreshadowing in *Coraline* include when Coraline sees a shadow of herself appear as a 'thin giant woman' (p.20) in Chapter 1, predicting the other mother, and when the neighbours pass on warnings from the mice and the tea-leaves.

Repetition

The repetition of some words and phrases is used to create a particular effect. For example, the repetition of 'for ever and always' helps to build a sense of unease (p.56, p.57, p.58, p.151). The other mother says it as though it is something Coraline should desire, almost as a parody of 'happily ever after' in a fairy tale; however, the prospect of 'for ever' with the other mother is alarming and the repetition of the phrase makes it feel sinister.

The repetition of 'only' during the introduction of the other mother emphasises the uncomfortable differences between her and Coraline's real mother. This also helps create a sense of unease:

> Only ...
> Only her skin was white as paper.
> Only she was taller and thinner.
> Only her fingers were too long ... (p.38)

Figurative language

Figurative language – including similes, metaphors, personification and onomatopoeia – is used to convey particular tones and create evocative images.

Similes are used frequently in the narrative's descriptive language to achieve different effects. For example, the ghosts are described as 'faint and pale as a moon in the daytime sky' (p.99), emphasising their strangeness and fragility, while the other mother is described as having teeth 'as sharp as knives' (p.149), conveying a sense of danger.

Metaphors have a similar descriptive function. For example, the cat explains the smallness of the other world with the statement: 'Spiders' webs only have to be large enough to catch flies' (p.90), suggesting that the other mother has constructed the world like a web to catch Coraline. **Personification**, which is the attribution of human qualities to animals or objects, for instance through the use of metaphor, is also used. When the house is deteriorating in the other world, Coraline thinks it seems to be 'crouching and staring down at her' (p.122) as if it is a person with unfriendly intentions, which gives it a menacing quality. The toys in the other world are also given human-like qualities – they sleep (p.80) and 'fluttered excitedly' at the sight of her (p.112) – conveying their magical, lifelike natures.

Onomatopoeia, the use of a word that sounds like the noise it represents, is another descriptive language tool. For example, Mr Bobo describes his mouse circus with terms such as *'toodle oodle'* (p.12, p.183). The word *'chink'* (p.36) is used to indicate the sound of keys falling; 'clunk' describes the sound of a key turning in the door (p.37, p.71, p.151); *'plop'* is used to describe the sound of things falling in the well (p.14); and *'t-t-t-t-t-t'* and *'kreeee … / … aaaak'* (p.19) help create an eerie atmosphere when Coraline hears strange noises at night.

Illustrations

There are several visual adaptations of *Coraline*, including a graphic novel, an illustrated tenth anniversary edition and a stop-motion film. Each of these provides a different visual interpretation and experience of the story. The edition under discussion in this text guide includes the original illustrations that accompanied the novel when it was first published in 2002. These consist of several full-page black-and-white images by Dave McKean, who has illustrated a number of Gaiman's stories.

These illustrations usually occur around the beginning of each chapter and represent significant moments in each. They are sketchy and shadowy in style, and they help to convey a particular tone. For example, the action scene of the cat about to land on the other mother's face (p.152) captures a moment of great tension, and the image of a mouse circus at the end of the novel conveys a sense of whimsy and peace.

CHAPTER-BY-CHAPTER ANALYSIS

Chapter 1 (pp.11–21)

Summary: *Coraline explores the grounds of the old house; when she stays inside due to poor weather, she discovers a door in the drawing room that opens to a brick wall; she follows a shadow into the room and dreams of small black shapes singing an ominous song.*

Chapter 1 introduces Coraline's world, including her parents, the subdivided old house she has recently moved into, its grounds and her new neighbours. Although the neighbours are friendly, they seem eccentric and are preoccupied with their own interests – Miss Spink and Miss Forcible's pet dogs and their pasts as 'famous actresses' (p.12), and the mouse circus of the 'crazy old man' (p.12, p.14). They also all mispronounce Coraline's name as 'Caroline' even after she corrects them, suggesting they have little interest in her. Coraline's parents are busy working and dismiss her, indicating they find her bothersome; they tell her to 'pester' the neighbours (p.14) and 'leave [them] alone to work' (p.16).

Coraline explores the house and grounds alone, demonstrating her interest in adventure. She looks for animals and seems intrigued by various creatures or items, such as 'a hedgehog', 'a snakeskin' and 'a rock that looked just like a frog' (p.14). She also seeks out a 'dangerous' well after she is warned away from it, telling herself this will help her 'keep away from it properly' (p.13) – an excuse she makes because she wants to find the well. This suggests that she is unafraid of risk, and that she is happy to twist the truth for her own purposes.

Key point

Many seemingly unimportant moments in this chapter set up events that later become significant. These include Coraline seeing a 'haughty black cat' (p.14); finding the well; feeling 'bored with her toys' (p.15); being annoyed with her father's 'recipe' (p.18); and watching the television program that teaches her about 'protective coloration' (p.15), which helps her in Chapter 13.

After Coraline's mother unlocks the drawing-room door, events in the chapter become more ominous. Coraline sees shapes moving into the room, described in terms relating to vermin ('scuttled', 'spider', p.19); her shadow distorts into 'a thin giant woman' (p.20); she finds the door inexplicably ajar (p.20); and she dreams of small black shapes singing a threatening song (pp.20–1). These eerie images suggest Coraline's mother has released something frightening, and foreshadow the characters of the other mother and the rats, whom Coraline will soon meet.

Key vocabulary

trod the boards (p.12): performed as a theatre actor.

protective coloration (p.15): an animal's colouring or patterning (e.g. camouflage) that helps its chances of survival.

Q How do you think Coraline feels about her neighbours? Which parts of the narration give you this impression?

Q How does the language used to describe Coraline's dream convey a sense of danger and unease?

Chapter 2 (pp.23–31)

Summary: *Coraline walks around the misty grounds and speaks to her neighbours; the old man passes on a message from the mice; Coraline has tea with Miss Spink and Miss Forcible, who tell her she is in danger; Miss Spink gives Coraline a stone with a hole in it.*

This chapter continues to set up events that occur later in the novel. Coraline's assertion that she is 'an explorer' (p.24) and the description of the mist creating a 'ghost-world' (p.31) foreshadow her explorations of the other world, which is later revealed to contain ghosts and supernatural mist-like 'nothingness' (p.87).

The old man's message from the mice, *'Don't go through the door'* (p.25), suggests something foreboding lies behind the drawing-room door. The fact that the mice somehow know about the door and say Coraline's name correctly ('They got your name wrong … They kept saying Coraline', pp.25–6), indicates that they should be taken seriously.

Miss Spink and Miss Forcible read Coraline's tea-leaves (a method of fortune-telling) and warn her she is in danger, though their advice consists of unhelpful superstitions from the theatre world. However, the stone Miss Spink gives her for protection becomes significant in later chapters.

The warnings from the mice and the tea-leaves reinforce the growing sense that something perilous has been put into motion since Coraline's mother unlocked the door.

Key vocabulary

wellington boots (p.23): waterproof boots often made of rubber; another name for gumboots.

Portia (p.23): a character in Shakespeare's play *The Merchant of Venice*.

Ophelia (p.23): a character in Shakespeare's play *Hamlet*.

shingles (p.24): a condition that causes a painful rash. It is more common in older people.

Scottie (p.27): a nickname for the Scottish terrier dog breed (a kind of Highland terrier).

bone-china (p.28): a type of porcelain made from clay mixed with bone ash.

Garibaldi biscuit (p.28): a type of biscuit consisting of currants sandwiched between thin layers of biscuit dough.

Madame Arcati (p.28): a character in the play *Blithe Spirit* by Noël Coward.

Lady Bracknell (p.28): a character in the play *The Importance of Being Earnest* by Oscar Wilde.

don't wear green in your dressing room (p.30): a reference to a superstition among theatre actors that wearing green will cause bad luck.

[don't] mention the Scottish play (p.30): a reference to a theatre superstition that saying the name of Shakespeare's play *Macbeth* will cause bad luck. Those who believe the superstition call it 'the Scottish play' to avoid saying the name.

Q Coraline thinks danger is 'exciting' rather than 'a bad thing' (p.31). What does this tell us about her? What other things does she say or do that reinforce this characterisation?

Chapter 3 (pp.33–44)

Summary: *Coraline goes clothes shopping with her mother; at home, she unlocks the drawing-room door and discovers a hallway; she goes through it and meets the other mother, the other father, the rats and the other old man upstairs.*

Even while shopping for Coraline's clothes, her mother pays little attention to Coraline. She ignores what Coraline says, including her request for green gloves, and discusses what to buy with the shop assistant instead.

Coraline's boredom drives her to unlock the drawing-room door, which leads her to the other world. It appears similar to her own, but details and language choices emphasise its differences in a way that creates a sense of menace and unease. A boy in a picture looks as though he is 'planning to do something very nasty' to some bubbles; the other mother is described as having unnatural and unpleasant features such as 'curved and sharp' fingernails, and fingers that 'never stopped moving'; and the people have black buttons for eyes (p.38).

However, Coraline finds aspects of this world intriguing or enjoyable. She enjoys lunch, contrasting with her disgust at the 'recipe' her father cooked in Chapter 1 (p.18). The other parents are attentive, and her bedroom contains 'remarkable things' (p.41), unlike her real flat, where she is 'bored with her toys' and has 'read all her books' (p.15).

The other mother's suggestion that Coraline play 'with the rats' (p.40) is an unusual one that highlights the uncomfortable sense that something is wrong with her and this world, and Coraline's meeting with the rats brings back the atmosphere of unease. Their 'red eyes', tails like 'long, smooth worms' and pyramid formation create an unnerving image (p.42). Their song echoes the one from her dream, and similarly carries a sense of threat, emphasising the rats' '*teeth*', '*tails*' and '*eyes*' (p.42). The rats scampering on the other old man is another discomforting image, with 'restless lumps … sliding' beneath his clothes (p.43). Coraline's glimpse of 'something hungry in the old man's button eyes' (p.43) suggests he may have dangerous motivations.

Coraline leaves the house as her other parents farewell her, 'smiling identical smiles, and waving slowly' (p.44). Although they give her more attention than her real parents do, she does not seem comfortable with this level of focus, which feels almost sinister.

Key vocabulary

Day-glo (p.33): the company DayGlo manufactures florescent pigments. The 'Day-glo green gloves' Coraline wants would be a bright green.

pullover (p.33): another word for jumper.

Q Coraline asks for green gloves because '*everybody* at school's got grey blouses' but '*nobody's* got green gloves' (p.33). What does this tell us about Coraline and the things she values?

Chapter 4 (pp.45–59)

Summary: *Coraline speaks with the cat; she watches the other Miss Spink and Miss Forcible perform; the other mother and father ask to replace her eyes with buttons; Coraline returns home.*

The cat Coraline saw in Chapter 1 can speak here, perhaps telepathically ('its voice sounded like the voice at the back of Coraline's head', p.45). It seems the cat can travel between the worlds without using the hallway, suggesting a different kind of relationship with the other world.

The other Miss Spink and Miss Forcible's flat is a theatre, where they appear as young women with button eyes. Their various performances include circus activities and Shakespearean quotes, and their staff and audience are talking dogs. There are clear links here to the real Miss Spink and Miss Forcible, who frequently refer to their youth as actors, and own many dogs. However, the other Miss Spink and Miss Forcible are young performers in their prime, unlike the real neighbours, who are retired, don't make 'any sense' to Coraline (p.30) and say her name incorrectly (whereas the other Miss Spink knows it before Coraline tells her: 'Coraline ... what's your name?', p.53). Like the other mother's cooking and the bedroom with 'remarkable things' (p.41), this flat of endless, exciting performances promises to replace an aspect of Coraline's world with something more desirable.

The other parents reveal that they want to replace Coraline's eyes with buttons in exchange for her staying with them 'for ever and always' (p.57). The strangeness and enormity of this request contradicts the assertion that they will be 'one big happy family' (p.58) – real parents would not ask their children to undergo such a painful, invasive procedure. Coraline's behaviour indicates her discomfort: she tells the other mother not to touch her hair and backs away.

Key point

This chapter demonstrates the importance of the stone with a hole in it. The cat tells her she was sensible to bring 'protection' (p.49), foreshadowing the stone's power. Coraline touches the stone while deciding whether to stay (p.57), which suggests it had some influence in her choosing to leave. The other mother's hand reacts 'like a frightened spider' (p.58) when Coraline touches the stone, as though its power repels her. This, alongside Miss Spink's earlier assertion that it is 'good for bad things' (pp.30–1), implies that the other mother is a 'bad thing'.

Language and imagery contribute to a tense atmosphere, reiterating the danger of the other world. The other mother's hair drifting 'like plants under the sea' (p.58) suggests that she is not human. The passageway between worlds is described in frightening, Gothic terms: 'strange voices whispered and distant winds howled ... there was something in the dark' (p.59). In contrast, the language describing Coraline's return to her flat is concrete and straightforward, conveying a sense of safety and relief: 'She was home' (p.59).

Key vocabulary

anteroom (p.50): a small room that leads to a larger room.

gramophone needle (p.53): the needle that picks up sound from the grooves in a record.

addendum (p.53): addition.

Q Why does Coraline reject the other mother and other father?

Chapter 5 (pp.61–80)

Summary: *Coraline waits for her parents; the cat takes her to see them in a mirror; she calls the police; she tells the cat a story about her father's bravery; they return to the other world; the other mother takes the key; the cat advises Coraline to challenge the other mother.*

Coraline's attempts to look after herself without her parents indicate her youthfulness – she eats insubstantial meals such as 'a block of cooking chocolate and an apple' (p.62). She cries and sleeps in her parents' room, indicating she feels deeply unhappy without them. The adults Coraline speaks to demonstrate the same dismissive attitudes she has experienced previously: Miss Spink and Miss Forcible ignore her alarming statement that her parents have 'vanished under mysterious circumstances' (p.63), and the police officer unhelpfully suggests she ask her mother for 'hot chocolate' and a 'hug' (p.67), assuming she is simply recounting a nightmare.

The cat doesn't speak in the real world; however, by showing Coraline the mirror with her parents, it indicates it wants to help her. Coraline recounts a story about her father saving her from wasps, which informs her definition of bravery: 'when you're scared but you still do it anyway' (p.72). Although she is afraid, she will be brave and return to the other world, demonstrating her deep love for her real mother and father.

The atmosphere in the passageway is frightening. The candle goes out 'as if it had been snuffed' and there are sounds with unknown sources – 'a scrabbling and a pattering' (p.73). The sense of danger is reiterated when Coraline sees her other parents, who look at her 'hungrily' (p.74), while the other mother's non-human features are highlighted: her teeth are 'too long' and her hair drifts 'like the tentacles of a creature in the deep ocean', suggesting a predatorial nature (p.75). This casts doubt on the truthfulness of her offer: 'We're ready to love you and play with you and … make your life interesting' (p.73).

Despite the other mother's sinister appearance, her behaviour towards Coraline is familiar in some ways, echoing how the adults in Coraline's world have dismissed or spoken down to her. When accused by Coraline of stealing her parents, the other mother calls her 'silly' (p.75), and she tells the other father not to 'bother our darling Coraline's head' when he informs her that there is just one key for the door between worlds (p.77). Coraline eating an apple instead of accepting the other parents' food is an assertion of self-reliance and a rejection of the other mother's attempt to position her as the child in her vision of a family (p.74). The cat's description of the other mother as a creature that 'wants something to love' or 'something to eat' (p.79) reinforces the notion that she is not human and has dangerous motivations.

Coraline's realisation that the other parents' bedroom 'would remain empty until the exact moment that she opened the door' (p.80) indicates her understanding that the other world is one big illusion, designed specifically for her.

Key point

Mirrors play an important role in this chapter, revealing both truth and illusion. Coraline's parents appear trapped behind a mirror, and Coraline takes comfort in seeing her reflection in the mirror in the other world and noting she is still her own person – her eyes are 'real eyes, not black buttons' (p.74). However, this mirror also shows a lie: the other mother's illusion of Coraline's parents demonstrates her significant powers of manipulation and deception. The mirror features later in the novel, including when it doesn't show the other mother's reflection (p.92); when Coraline is trapped behind it and meets the ghost children in Chapter 7; and when it reflects a trail of green fire in the direction of the first soul (p.112). The mirror motif suggests the other world is a warped kind of 'mirror' to Coraline's real world.

Key vocabulary

Glasgow Empire press clippings (p.62): the Glasgow Empire Theatre in Glasgow, Scotland, closed in 1963. Miss Spink has clippings from the press about the theatre, such as excerpts from old newspapers.

Royal Tunbridge Wells (p.63): a town in England.

Q Why do you think the world seems to 'shimmer a little at the edges' (p.75) when Coraline states she wants her parents back?

Chapter 6 (pp.81–95)

Summary: *Coraline speaks to the other father; she discovers a snow-globe with two people in it; she explores the other world; the other mother locks her behind a mirror.*

The clothing in Coraline's room, like many features of the other world, appears designed to appeal to her, including costumes and clothes made of unique materials. When she puts the stone in her pocket, however, she feels she has emerged from 'fog' (p.84), suggesting it is protecting her from being taken in by the apparent charms of this world.

The other father seems lonely, 'pleased to have somebody to talk to' (p.84). He also appears 'less like her true father today' (p.84), indicating that the illusion is slipping. The revelation that the other mother created this world and its people is proof that nothing in this world is true, and Coraline's explorations are also evidence of this. The further she walks, the less real everything appears, until she is walking through 'a pale nothingness' (p.87), before the house magically reappears before her. As she walks, the cat plays with a rat, pretending to let it escape. This foreshadows the game that the other mother and Coraline will soon play, comparing the predatory natures of the cat and the other mother and alluding to Coraline's position as the 'prey' that gets to 'escape' (p.91).

The chapter concludes with Coraline being locked behind a mirror. The other mother's speech here reflects common chastisements mothers might give when disciplining their children ('Is that any way to talk to your mother?', p.93; 'For your own good', p.95); however, her lack of real maternal authority highlights the absurdity of the situation and her manipulative character. As with the other father, the illusion is slipping – 'she seemed taller than Coraline remembered' (p.94).

Several moments in this chapter allude to the notion of the other mother as a spider and the other world as a spider's web, including the other mother eating beetles (p.93) and the cat's metaphor: 'Spiders' webs only have to be large enough to catch flies' (p.90). See the section on the other mother in 'Characters & relationships' for more details.

Key vocabulary

sharper than a serpent's tooth (p.92): a reference to a line from Shakespeare's play *King Lear*. The full quote is, 'How sharper than a serpent's tooth it is / To have a thankless child.'

manners makyth man (p.95): an old proverb meaning that good manners are deeply important.

Q Why does the other father call the cat, rather than the rats, 'vermin' (p.84)?

Q How does the narrative so far suggest that the other mother has more authority or power than the other father?

Chapter 7 (pp.96–103)

Summary: *Coraline meets three ghost children, who warn her to flee; they ask Coraline to free their souls and tell her to look through the stone.*

The ghost children's dialogue includes old-fashioned phrases such as 'art thou' (p.97), indicating that they are from a different time and have been trapped for many decades. Descriptions of the ghost children emphasise indistinctness – they are 'nothing more than afterimages' (p.101), with 'faint' and 'wispy' voices (p.103).

They remember glimpses of their past lives, but little about their identities as living children, and have forgotten their names. Their warning that the other mother will steal Coraline's heart and soul is chilling; it is clear that their fate is what awaits Coraline should the other mother succeed. Despite these horrifying revelations, Coraline behaves with pragmatism, reasoning that the other mother will take her out 'to play games' (p.102). This demonstrates Coraline's bravery and determination in the face of great danger.

Key vocabulary

hoop and stick (p.97): used in an old-fashioned children's game.

scullery (p.100): a small room next to a kitchen, traditionally found in older, more expensive houses, used for tasks such as cleaning dishes and laundering.

peradventure (p.101): an old term meaning 'perhaps'.

Q When one of the ghosts recalls that it may have been a boy, it glows 'a little more brightly' (p.99). Why do you think this happens? What does this suggest?

Chapter 8 (pp.105–21)

Summary: *The other mother releases Coraline from behind the mirror, and Coraline challenges her to a game; the other mother accepts and swears on her right hand; Coraline finds two of the ghost children's souls.*

The other mother continues to try to control Coraline through her pretence of parental authority: 'if you will be a good child … you and I shall understand each other perfectly and we shall love each other perfectly as well' (p.106). However, we now know that giving in to the other mother will have catastrophic consequences. Coraline's proposal of a game shows her resourcefulness, providing a way for her to escape, rescue her parents and free the ghost children.

When Coraline looks through the stone, her surroundings appear 'grey and colourless, like a pencil drawing' except for the soul (p.114), suggesting both that the stone has a magical, truth-revealing quality, and that the soul is the only thing 'real' here. The fact that the first soul had been at the bottom of the toybox – a place the narrative describes as being for 'forgotten objects, abandoned and unloved' (p.113) – reflects the way in which the other mother has discarded the ghost children, like a child who has become distracted by a new toy. Coraline's decision to wear her pyjamas rather than the clothes from the other world illustrates her determination to behave independently. The ghost child's warning that the beldam is angry indicates that the other mother knows what is happening, even when she is not present herself. Coraline's sensation of stinging sand (p.115) demonstrates this anger, as well as the extent of the other mother's control over the environment.

The theatre is significantly different from the one Coraline encountered in her first visit. It appears 'derelict and abandoned' with 'old, dusty spiders' webs' and 'rotten wood' (p.117), creating an atmosphere of deterioration. Instead of a lively audience of dogs, there are 'hairless, jellyish' bat-like 'things' (p.117) – a grotesque image suggesting these creatures, like the theatre, have degenerated.

The other Miss Spink and Miss Forcible similarly appear much more monstrous than before, and are described with allusions to bugs and insects (e.g. 'like a slug', 'like a spider's egg-case', p.118; 'like a ... bluebottle', p.120), reiterating the notion of this world as a web, controlled by the spider-like other mother. The language also suggests that there is something undeveloped about them: 'horribly unformed and unfinished, as if two Plasticine people had been warmed and rolled together' (p.118), 'like two lumps of wax' (p.120). References to these materials, known for their mouldable qualities, hint at the characters' manufactured nature. Like their surroundings, they were created by the other mother, and are rapidly unravelling. The discomfort of this imagery not only heightens the sense of grotesque horror, but also emphasises the falseness of the playful world from before.

Q There are several visceral sensations described during Coraline's recovery of the second soul. Find some examples. How do they contribute to the atmosphere in the chapter?

Chapter 9 (pp.122–33)

Summary: *The other mother gives Coraline a key to the empty flat; Coraline discovers the creature that had been the other father; it tries to attack her and she narrowly escapes.*

The other world appears as a 'formless, swirling mist' (p.122), a deterioration indicating that Coraline's actions are disrupting it. The other mother's voice emanating from 'the mist, and the fog, and the house, and the sky' (p.124) points to her connection to the world, and suggests she is losing control over where her voice is coming from – both she and the world she has created are falling apart. Her love for Coraline, which Coraline characterises as resembling how 'a miser loves money, or a dragon loves its gold', is an inherently negative kind of love revolving around control and 'possession' (p.124). Coraline whistles to manage her fear, demonstrating her courage and perseverance.

The empty flat, like the theatre, has an atmosphere of deterioration: the light switch is 'rusting', the cellar walls are 'flaking' and the rubbish includes 'mildewed papers, and decaying curtains' (p.128). Like the other Miss Forcible and Miss Spink, the other father has become monstrous – no longer a person but a 'thing' (p.129). It is described in terms that reference bugs ('pale and swollen, like a grub', p.129) as well as in terms that emphasise a sense of incompleteness ('puffed and swollen like risen bread dough', 'pale clay', p.129). The reference to bread dough echoes the description of the other father in Chapter 6 ('bread dough that had begun to rise', p.85), suggesting that the other father's shifting form is a continuation of a process that had begun earlier. Like the wax and the Plasticine, the role of dough and clay as materials used to make other things emphasises the other father's nature as a creation. Coraline's inability to see the other father through the stone highlights this lack of substance, contrasting with the vibrant colour of the children's souls. The only features that are still recognisable are the black-button eyes, a symbol of the other mother's ownership.

The other father also reflects the faintness of the ghost children. It whispers, speaks 'indistinctly', looks around 'vacantly', and tells her there is 'nothing but dust and damp and forgetting' (p.130), reminiscent of the ghost children's struggle to remember themselves. Just as the ghost children were trapped and abandoned, the other father has been created and discarded – 'a thing she made and then threw away' (p.130).

Despite this, it appears to hold values of its own and warns Coraline away, although it also seems to be under the control of the other mother and can't fully act on its own values: it pauses 'as if it was being told what to do' (p.132). When it attacks, it is described in terms that bring to mind the movements of monsters or animals: 'the thing twisted bonelessly ... its toothless mouth opened wide' (p.131); '[it] flopped and writhed, hunting for her'; 'fast as a serpent, it slithered for the steps' (p.132).

Coraline escapes by blinding the creature and sneaking out, highlighting her quick thinking. Afterwards, she 'hugged herself, and told herself that she was brave' (p.133), as though imitating the way her parents might comfort her, if they were present.

Key vocabulary

miser (p.124): someone who hoards their wealth.

Q Why do you think Coraline enters the empty flat, knowing the other mother is likely planning a trick?

Chapter 10 (pp.134–46)

Summary: *The other old man tries to persuade Coraline to stay and disintegrates into a mass of rats when she refuses; the cat kills the rat carrying the third soul; Coraline figures out where her parents are, picks up the cat and goes to confront the other mother.*

The rats' threatening song (p.135) is a reprise of the ones Coraline heard in Chapter 3 and in her dream in Chapter 1. Like the others, it emphasises the rats' features, such as tails and teeth, and suggests some kind of uprising. The language associated with the rats is unsettling, alluding to something ominous and unseen – 'shadows at the edges of things' (p.135). The flat smelling of 'rotten' food (p.135) conveys a sense of decay similar to that in the theatre and the cellar holding the other father, reiterating the notion that the world is unravelling. Coraline realises that everything is a 'ghastly parody' of the things and people in the real world (p.137). This shift in her perspective enables her to stop feeling afraid and helps her determine where her parents are hidden.

The other old man's voice reminds Coraline of an 'enormous dead insect' (p.137), continuing the metaphor of the other mother as a spider, surrounded by bug-like creatures. Although he is unsettling, speaking 'from the shadows' (p.138), he doesn't present much physical danger. He is described repeatedly as a 'voice' in ways that separate him from his body. Along with references to his voice being 'dead' (p.137, p.140), this foreshadows his disintegration into a mass of rats.

He makes a last effort to convince Coraline to stay, in a discussion that heavily references early chapters of the novel: 'You'll be bored. You'll be ignored. No one will listen to you … They don't even get your name right' (p.138). His promise of a world designed 'all for you' (p.138) highlights the fact that the other world and its inhabitants were built specifically to entice Coraline. Coraline makes similar references to ideas in earlier chapters, asking if there will be 'awful meals … made from recipes' and times when 'the day drags on forever' (p.138), indicating she understands how the other old man and, by extension, the other mother are trying to persuade her to stay. Coraline's refusal reveals her outlook on life overall, and her acknowledgement that 'meaning' (p.139) is more important than having things represents a high level of maturity.

Key point

Coraline's decision is representative of her transitioning from childhood to young adulthood. Although she is young and places value on toys, attention and excitement, she is mature enough to know the value of finding meaning in her own accomplishments, rather than having things handed to her. In this way, her refusal to stay is representative of her growth and her steps away from childhood. This growth contrasts with the other mother who, able to shape the world as she pleases, is accustomed to having whatever (and whoever) she wants.

The other old man's disintegration echoes the ways in which the other mother's world is falling to pieces. The environment similarly continues to disintegrate, becoming like 'a photograph' (p.141) and then a 'scribble' (p.144), indicating a rapid pace of change. Coraline's act of defiance seems to have been a blow to the already unstable world.

Key vocabulary

pell-mell (p.141): in a disorderly way.

Q Find examples of interesting or evocative language use. How do these help describe the characters, setting or narrative events?

Chapter 11 (pp.147–58)

Summary: *Coraline tricks the other mother into unlocking the door; she throws the cat at her, takes the snow-globe and runs into the corridor; the ghost children and her parents' encouragement help her to close the door, though 'something' falls into the corridor (p.155); Coraline escapes back to her flat with the cat.*

The other mother appears terrifying – 'huge … the colour of a spider's belly' with hair that 'writhed and twined' and teeth 'sharp as knives' (p.149). Like the deteriorating environment, her power is faltering and she cannot disguise herself anymore.

Coraline's mother's words, 'Well done, Coraline', enable Coraline to close the door, 'easily as anything' (p.155). This demonstrates the power of supportive, meaningful connections, in contrast to the possessive 'love' of the other mother. Coraline traverses the corridor for the last time. Note that each time Coraline travels through the corridor, it is described for longer, in more detail, and appears more frightening – changes that suggest there is something supernatural about it and that it is becoming more dangerous each time she goes through. In this final journey, the corridor conveys a particular sense of aliveness and danger – the wall is covered in fur and moves 'as if it were taking a breath' (p.156); it is 'older by far than the other mother' (pp.156–7) and somehow knows that Coraline is there (p.157). These descriptions contribute to a tense atmosphere and hint at unknown dangers even more terrifying than the other mother.

When Coraline returns to her flat, the imagery and descriptive language demonstrate the ways in which she has changed. She focuses on the beauty of the world – 'golden late-afternoon daylight', the 'robin's-egg blue' sky, 'green hills, which faded on the horizon into purples and greys' and 'rich sunlight' that turns the cat's whiskers 'gold' (p.158). This heightened language reflects a sense of wonder, contrasting with the language used to describe the empty 'white mist-light' (p.158) and decay of the other world, and her persistent boredom with the real world in earlier chapters. This changed perspective implies Coraline's relief to be out of the other world, as well as a deep, newfound appreciation of her home.

Q How do the physical descriptions of the other mother in this chapter contribute to her characterisation?

Chapter 12 (pp.159–69)

Summary: *Coraline spends time with her parents; she dreams of the ghost children, who warn her about the other mother; she wakes to find the other mother's hand searching for the passageway key.*

The snow-globe is now empty of people, indicating that Coraline's parents are now free. Despite disliking her father's cooking, Coraline eats most of her dinner and shows affection towards her parents, illustrating her appreciation of them after her ordeal.

In the dream, the ghost children appear in vivid detail, contrasting with their faintness in the other world. This suggests that, now free, they can reclaim their past identities, which they previously struggled to recall. Their appearances and speech patterns also convey information about these past lives; the boy and tall girl wear outdated clothing and use overtly old-fashioned language. The third ghost child has wings and eats flowers, suggesting the other mother has been stealing supernatural as well as human children. The ghost children traversing a bridge towards 'uncharted lands' (p.166) represents their crossing of the divide between the world of the living and of the dead, releasing them from limbo.

The other mother's hand is described in terms of vermin. Coraline wonders if it is 'a rat with an extra leg' (p.168), and its movements and appearance are spider-like: it 'scuttled' on 'long white legs' and has 'too-many tapping, clicking, scurrying feet' (p.169). These descriptions, along with its behaviour, 'reaching and clutching and snatching' (p.169), create a threatening, animalistic image. The hand's colours also convey a sense of threat: 'crimson-nailed', the flesh 'the colour of bone' (p.169).

Key vocabulary

staging post (p.166): a stopping point in a longer journey.

Q The tall girl notes that 'the beldam swore by her good right hand … but she lied' (p.166). What is the significance of this?

Chapter 13 (pp.171–85)

Summary: *Coraline protects the key and considers how to get rid of the other mother's hand; she sets up a picnic with dolls over the well and tricks the hand into falling into it; Mr Bobo's mice play instruments as Coraline falls asleep.*

Miss Forcible's tea-leaf reading, revealing a hand-shaped clump of leaves, and her dog's injury, indicate that the hand still presents a danger. The old man upstairs, whom Coraline soon learns is called Mr Bobo, also tells Coraline that the mice are frightened.

Coraline sets up a picnic with dolls as 'protective coloration' (p.175), a phenomenon she learned about in Chapter 1. By pretending to be playing like a young child to lure the hand, she demonstrates her ability to 'be tricky' (p.167), as the ghost children suggested.

After Coraline traps the hand, Mr Bobo listens, for the first time, when Coraline corrects his mispronunciation of her name. Coraline returns the stone and goes to bed, realising she is not frightened about the first day of school like she usually is, suggesting she has grown through the events of the novel. She hears the mice playing instruments as she falls asleep.

Q What is the significance of both Mr Bobo and Coraline learning each other's names in this chapter?

CHARACTERS & RELATIONSHIPS

Coraline Jones

Key quotes

'*In danger*? thought Coraline to herself. It sounded exciting.' (p.31)

'I'm going back for them because they are my parents. And if they noticed I was gone I'm sure they would do the same for me ...' (p.72)

'"You really don't understand, do you?" she said. "I don't *want* whatever I want. Nobody does. Not really. What kind of fun would it be if I just got everything I ever wanted? Just like that, and it didn't *mean* anything. What then?"' (p.139)

Coraline is an adventurous young girl who thinks of herself as an explorer. She appreciates interesting and unusual things and likes the idea of standing out, arguing that she 'could be the only one' wearing green gloves at school (p.33). She considers the prospect of danger 'exciting' (p.31), and goes through the door to the other world despite the mice and the tea-leaves warning her against it.

While Coraline initially feels unhappy with aspects of her life, bored with the school holidays and ignored by the adults around her, she still doesn't agree to leaving her family and staying in the other world. She places great value on her independence and ability to find meaning for herself and, towards the end of the novel, shows appreciation for the life she has (see 'Growing up' in 'Themes, ideas & values' for further discussion).

Coraline also demonstrates great bravery and perseverance. Although she frequently feels afraid during her second trip to the other world, she still pushes herself onwards, and defines bravery as 'when you're scared but you still do it anyway' (p.72). She is highly intelligent, and uses her quick thinking to escape the other world and trick the other mother's hand into falling into the well. One of the ghost children tells her she has the 'blessings' of 'good fortune and wisdom and courage' (p.167).

Coraline shows care and compassion to others: she faces great danger to rescue her parents and recover the souls of the three ghost children, and ensures the cat makes it safely out of the other world.

Mr and Mrs Jones

Key quotes

'Why don't you go and bother Miss Spink and Miss Forcible?' (Mr Jones, p.27)

'And while I was running up the hill, my dad stayed and got stung, to give me time to run away.' (Coraline, p.70)

'And then a voice that sounded like her mother's – her own mother, her real, wonderful, maddening, infuriating, glorious mother, just said, "Well done, Coraline," and that was enough.' (pp.154–5)

Coraline's parents initially don't pay much attention to her, and annoy her at several points. They are too busy working to play with her; her mother disregards her opinion when buying her school clothes, and her father cooks complicated 'recipes' (p.19) that she doesn't like.

Despite this, Coraline shares a deep bond with her parents, and does not hesitate to rescue them from the other mother despite the danger to herself. They similarly care deeply for her. Coraline's father once let himself get stung by wasps to help her escape them, which informs her understanding of what it means to be brave. Coraline's mother's voice gives Coraline the strength to close the passageway door against the other mother, demonstrating the strong influence of her encouragement for Coraline. Coraline is more affectionate towards both her parents after rescuing them.

April Spink and Miriam Forcible

Key quote

'"I played Portia once," said Miss Spink. "Miss Forcible talks about her Ophelia, but it was my Portia they came to see ..."' (p.23)

Miss Spink and Miss Forcible are two old women who live in the ground-floor flat with their pet dogs. They were actors when they were young, which seems important to them: many of their discussions revolve around the theatre, and their flat is decorated with old theatre programs and photos from their youth.

They are friendly to Coraline; however, they often don't listen to her. They call her 'Caroline' (e.g. p.11), and don't notice when she tells them her parents are missing (pp.62–3). Coraline in turn finds them somewhat difficult to understand and thinks they don't make 'any sense', a tendency she attributes to many adults (p.30).

They are also superstitious, and offer Coraline advice from theatre traditions such as 'don't wear green in your dressing room' (p.30). However, some of their beliefs appear to be true. Their tea-leaf readings accurately predict that Coraline is in danger and it is thanks to the stone with a hole in it, given to her by Miss Spink, that Coraline is able to locate the ghost children's souls and think clearly in the other world.

Mr Bobo ('the crazy old man upstairs')

Key quote

'"One day, little Caroline, when they are all ready, everyone in the whole world will see the wonders of my mouse circus. You ask me why you cannot see it now. Is that what you asked me?"
"No," said Coraline quietly, "I asked you not to call me Caroline. It's Coraline."' (p.12)

Mr Bobo is a friendly, eccentric old man who lives in the top flat and claims to be training a mouse circus. He speaks in an exuberant manner and is from an old circus family who, according to Miss Spink, are 'Romanian or Slovenian or Livonian, or [from] one of those countries' (p.178).

He passes on messages from the mice to Coraline as though they speak to him directly, and Coraline initially thinks he has made up the mouse circus. Mr Bobo doesn't learn Coraline's name until the final chapter. Although it annoys Coraline that the adults mispronounce her name, she similarly doesn't learn Mr Bobo's name until the end of the book, and had previously referred to him using the unflattering descriptors 'old' and 'crazy' (e.g. p.12). Coraline and Mr Bobo learning each other's names suggests that they are taking each other more seriously and will treat each other with more respect in the future.

The mice

Although she never sees them, the mice try to help Coraline by sending her messages – which are surprisingly accurate – through Mr Bobo. They tell her not to go through the door to the other world and say her name correctly, even though Mr Bobo thinks they are wrong ('They kept saying Coraline. Not Caroline', p.26). They fear the other mother, and call Coraline their 'saviour' (p.183) when she traps the other mother's hand.

The cat

Key quotes

'"I'm not the other anything. I'm me." It tipped its head on one side; green eyes glinted. "You people are spread all over the place. Cats, on the other hand, keep ourselves together ..."' (p.47)

'"We ... we could be friends, you know," said Coraline.
"We *could* be rare specimens of an exotic breed of African dancing elephants," said the cat. "But we're not ..."' (p.48)

Like Coraline, the cat – which the other mother and father refer to as 'vermin' (p.84, p.147) – has no 'other' version of itself. It appears as an ordinary black cat, but it can speak with Coraline, apparently telepathically, in the other world, and Coraline seems to be able to speak back to it with her thoughts on page 151 when they confront the other mother. It also has knowledge of the other world and other mother. In particular, it knows of the other mother's love of games ('her kind of thing loves games and challenges', p.79), and has an idea of her motivations: 'she wants something to love' or 'something to eat' (p.79). It can also travel between worlds without the passageway until Chapter 10 when 'the ways in and out' go 'flat' (p.145).

When Coraline first meets the cat, it appears arrogant and spurns her suggestion of friendship. Coraline initially finds it 'irritatingly self-centred' (p.48) and is horrified when it plays with a rat it has hunted. Its excuse – playing with food 'permits the occasional ... snack to escape' (p.91) – foreshadows the challenge between Coraline and the other mother.

The cat helps Coraline multiple times throughout the story. It helps her figure out that her parents are trapped in the other world, advises her to challenge the other mother and kills the rat holding a ghost child's soul. It also attacks the other mother when Coraline throws it at her. Through their shared ordeal, they come to consider each other friends, and it expresses joy when Coraline traps the other mother's hand.

The ghost children

Key quote

'She will take your life and all you are and all you care'st for, and she will leave you with nothing but mist and fog ... A husk you'll be, a wisp you'll be, and a thing no more than a dream on waking, or a memory of something forgotten.' (ghost child, pp.101–2)

The three ghost children represent what will happen to Coraline if she stays with the other mother. Coraline meets them trapped behind a mirror in the other world, and their stories are similar to Coraline's – one describes going through a door to find an 'other mamma' (p.100). The other mother kept their souls and fed on them until the children were 'only snakeskins and spiderhusks' (p.101). Coraline rescues each of their marble-shaped souls as part of her game with the other mother: one from the toybox, one from the other Miss Spink and Miss Forcible, and the third from one of the rats making up the other old man. When viewed through the stone, each soul has a different vibrant colour.

The children are initially described in terms that emphasise a sense of intangibility and otherworldliness: they are 'faint and pale as a moon in the daytime sky' (p.99). They use old-fashioned language such as 'art thou' and 'beldam' (p.97), have difficulty recalling their identities as living children and tell Coraline they have been trapped for a 'time beyond reckoning' (p.100).

They are much more clearly defined in Coraline's dream after she rescues their souls. The boy wears 'red-velvet knee-britches and a frilly white shirt', while the tall girl wears 'a brown, rather shapeless dress', suggesting she belongs to a less wealthy class (p.163). The third ghost child resembles some kind of fairy creature – she eats flowers, is dressed in 'what seemed to be spiders' webs, with a circle of glittering silver set in her blonde hair' and has 'two wings … coming out of her back' (p.164).

The high level of detail given to the ghost children in the dream suggests that, through their rescue, they can finally recall their past selves. These details also suggest the scope of the other mother's reach: she has been abducting children for a very long time, across classes and, in the case of the winged girl, even across species.

The other mother

Key quotes

'"Where are my parents?" Coraline asked.
"We're here," said her other mother, in a voice so close to her real mother's that Coraline could scarcely tell them apart. "We're here. We're ready to love you and play with you and feed you and make your life interesting."' (p.73)

'"She wants something to love, I think," said the cat. "Something that isn't her. She might want something to eat as well. It's hard to tell with creatures like that."' (p.79)

The other mother is the antagonist of the story: the creator of the other world and its button-eyed inhabitants. She is an ancient, powerful, manipulative and dangerous shapeshifter who traps and feeds on children. She claims to love Coraline, but seeks to control her entirely, as represented by her desire to replace Coraline's eyes with buttons. She discards those who are no longer useful to her, and when she is upset she 'takes it out on everybody else' (p.130). Many characters fear her, including the mice, cat, other father and ghost children, who call her 'the beldam' (e.g. p.97).

Her physical features include pale white skin, long fingers that move constantly, sharp nails and teeth, and hair that moves 'like ... tentacles' (p.75) or 'snakes' (p.105) – a description that links her to the ancient Greek monster Medusa, who has snakes for hair. She initially appears similar to Coraline's mother, except her nails are 'curved and sharp' (p.38), like the claws of an animal, and her teeth are 'a tiny bit too long' (p.75) – slight differences that present an uncomfortable sense of danger. As the story progresses and her illusions deteriorate, she becomes visibly more monstrous, particularly in Chapter 11, where she is 'huge' with teeth 'sharp as knives' and hair that 'writhed and twined about her head' (p.149).

Key point

The other mother is associated with spiders many times during the novel. She designed the other world to entrap Coraline by appealing to her desires (including attention, good food and interesting toys, demonstrating predatory behaviour akin to that of a spider laying out a web: 'She made it and she waited' (p.85). The cat uses a metaphor to make this comparison more explicit: 'Spiders' webs only have to be large enough to catch flies' (p.90). Coraline also feels something 'like a spider's web' (p.73) the second time she enters the other world.

There are references linking the other mother to spiders directly. Her hand 'scuttled ... like a frightened spider' (p.58); instead of sweets she eats 'blackbeetles' from a bag (p.93); when she appears at her most monstrous, she is 'the colour of a spider's belly' (p.149); and her hand later crawls around independently on its fingers, echoing the way spiders move on their legs.

→

The uncanny button eyes of the other mother and her creations – described as black, shiny, polished and sometimes hungry – recall the black eyes of spiders and insects. Further, her creations are described with language that associates them with insects: in a 'cocoon' (p.121); 'like a grub' (p.129); and with a voice that reminds Coraline of an 'enormous dead insect' (p.137). This implies that they are merely victims trapped in the other mother's web.

The other mother appears to want to take the place of Coraline's real mother and tries to make Coraline love her through force and manipulation (for more, see the section on love in 'Themes, ideas & values'). When Coraline defies her or makes progress with her challenge, it seems that the other world and its inhabitants deteriorate, indicating that when the other mother is displeased, her control over her world is weakened. When Coraline asks for her parents back, the world appears to 'shimmer' (p.75), and as Coraline recovers the ghost children's souls, the environment devolves further until it is a 'formless, swirling mist' (p.122).

Despite her great power, the other mother can only 'twist and copy and distort' existing things (p.137) – a fact that helps Coraline figure out that her parents are trapped in the snow-globe, as this item didn't have a counterpart in the real world.

The other father

Key quotes

'I shall demonstrate our tender hospitality to you, such that you will not even think about ever going back.' (p.85)

'In that dim light, it took her several seconds to recognise it for what it was: the thing was pale and swollen, like a grub, with thin, stick-like arms and feet. It had almost no features on its face, which had puffed and swollen like risen bread dough.' (p.129)

A creation of the other mother, the other father initially appears very similar to Coraline's father. He is not adept at deception and mistakenly reveals information to Coraline, telling her there is just one key between worlds, and that the other world was made by the other mother. The other mother locks him in the cellar as punishment for this.

Like the other creations, he devolves over time and becomes more monstrous, and more associated with insect imagery than human. In the other father's final appearance, the narrative uses the pronoun 'it' rather than 'he' to emphasise this change, and describes the creature as a 'thing' that is 'swollen, like a grub', with a 'mouthless face' (p.129). It is also likened to bread dough and clay, mouldable materials that emphasise its constructed nature: 'just a thing she made and then threw away' (p.130).

Despite the other mother's control over her creations, the other father's individual personality still shows through. When he appears as a human, he seems lonely, 'pleased to have somebody to talk to' (p.84), and when the other mother impels the 'grub-thing' to attack Coraline, it holds off for as long as it can and warns her to 'run' (p.131).

The other Miss Spink and Miss Forcible

Key quote

'Then they unbuttoned their fluffy round coats and opened them. But their coats weren't all that opened: their faces opened, too, like empty shells, and out of the old empty fluffy round bodies stepped two young women. They were thin, and pale, and quite pretty, and had black-button eyes.' (p.52)

The other Miss Spink and Miss Forcible first appear performing circus tricks and reciting lines from Shakespeare plays to a crowd of talking dogs. Unlike their real-world counterparts, they are in their prime, young and adored by their audience. Their flat appears as a theatre, likely intended to entice Coraline to stay in the other world.

Coraline's second visit shows the theatre 'derelict and abandoned', with the dogs as 'hairless, jellyish' creatures that hang upside-down from the ceiling (p.117). The other Miss Spink and Miss Forcible are in a 'sac' (p.118) together against the wall, and hold the second ghost child's soul. The descriptive language used here (e.g. 'like a spider's egg-case', p.118;

'like a spider's web', p.119; 'buzzed like a fat and angry bluebottle', p.120; 'cocoon', p.121) reiterates the spider and insect imagery of the other world. The women also appear merged together, which contributes to the atmosphere of horror and the idea of them being insects: 'a person with two heads, with twice as many arms and legs as it should have' (p.118). The references to them seeming like 'Plasticine' (p.118) and 'wax' (p.120) – mouldable materials – emphasise that they are creations.

The other 'crazy old man upstairs'

Key quote

'"Come here, little girl. I know what you want, little girl." It was a rustling voice, scratchy and dry. It made Coraline think of some kind of enormous dead insect.' (p.137)

The other old man is unnerving from the beginning. He wears rats beneath his clothing and watches Coraline with 'something hungry' in his button eyes (p.43). His speech patterns are distinct from the real old man's more exuberant manner of speaking – he says 'Hello, Coraline' (p.43), as opposed to the real old man's enthusiastic (and inaccurate) greetings (e.g. 'Ahoy! Caroline!', p.25) – highlighting the fact that, despite the visual similarities, the two are very different characters.

During Coraline's second visit to the other world, the other old man is substantially weakened – a 'voice', emanating from a figure in the dark, that makes Coraline think of a 'dead insect' (p.137), relating back to the insect imagery of all the 'other' characters. He makes a final attempt to persuade Coraline to stay: 'We will listen to you and play with you and laugh with you' (p.138). Upon Coraline's rejection, he falls apart into a number of rats, one of which carries the final soul.

THEMES, IDEAS & VALUES

Growing up

Key quotes

'"You really don't understand, do you?" she said. "I don't *want* whatever I want. Nobody does. Not really. What kind of fun would it be if I just got everything I ever wanted? Just like that, and it didn't *mean* anything. What then?"' (p.139)

'The sky had never seemed so *sky*; the world had never seemed so *world* … Nothing, she thought, had ever been so *interesting*.' (p.158)

Coraline's age positions her between the worlds of childhood and young adulthood – she is still young enough to need her parents to take care of her, but also old enough to wish for independence and individuality. One of the central themes of the book is Coraline's coming of age, and she experiences significant growth throughout the story.

The other mother and the other world

At the beginning of the novel, Coraline is unhappy with many aspects of her situation. On school holidays, she is 'bored with her toys' (p.15); her parents are too busy to play with her, and don't buy her the clothes she wants or cook her food she likes; and her neighbours don't listen to her and repeatedly mispronounce her name. Considering Coraline's frustrations, the other world seems uniquely suited to her. The toys are 'remarkable' (p.41); the adults are attentive; the clothes are of the kind 'she would love to have' (p.83); and she greatly enjoys the food (p.40). In this world, it seems, as the other old man tells her, she can have whatever she wants (p.139).

However, there is also a sense of stagnation in the other world. The eerie, repeated line of 'for ever and always' in Chapter 4 suggests that the other world will never change, and the other mother's idea of a permanent 'happy family' (p.58) will keep Coraline stuck in her role of child forever. The other mother also wants to control Coraline, to replace her eyes with buttons and force her to behave the way she likes: 'a good child who loves her mother … compliant and fair-spoken' (p.106). In this way, she seeks to undermine Coraline's autonomy, which is a crucial part of growing up, and to force her to stay in a static childish state forever, rather than go through the natural processes of growth and change.

Finding meaning and appreciating what one has

By the end of Coraline's ordeal in the other world, she knows what truly matters to her: not the superficial offerings of attention, toys and nice food, but her autonomy and the opportunity to find meaning for herself.

This is demonstrated in Chapter 10 when she says to the other old man: 'What kind of fun would it be if I just got everything I ever wanted … and it didn't *mean* anything. What then?' (p.139). The other old man's confusion – 'I don't understand' (p.139) – highlights his and the other mother's stagnated way of thinking. They don't understand the value of finding meaning in one's own life but rather place value on simply having things.

After Coraline returns home, she feels a renewed appreciation of what she already has, viewing the world around her with a sense of wonder: 'The sky had never seemed so *sky*; the world had never seemed so *world*' (p.158). She no longer focuses on her boredom or the things that had bothered her previously, and shows affection to her parents, even eating her father's cooking, indicating that she feels particularly thankful for them after almost losing them in the other world. She is also kinder to her neighbours, hugging Miss Spink and Miss Forcible and calling Mr Bobo by his name. This change in behaviour signals that she now perceives things differently, and has learned to value those around her, rather than thinking only of her own interests.

Finally, Coraline also feels more capable by the end of the novel. She doesn't feel nervous about the first day of school as she usually does, suggesting that her ordeals in the other world have helped her become more confident in her ability to face whatever the future holds.

Bravery

Key quotes

'"Because," she said, "when you're scared but you still do it anyway, *that's* brave."' (Coraline, p.72)

'I will be brave, thought Coraline. No, I *am* brave.' (p.74)

'"You don't frighten me," said Coraline, although they did frighten her, very much.' (p.75)

Overcoming fear is an integral aspect of Coraline's journey. Although she is initially unbothered by things that many might consider frightening (she actively seeks out the 'dangerous' well, p.13, and thinks that being in danger sounds 'exciting', p.31), after her parents are kidnapped Coraline is frequently afraid as she returns to the other world and faces the terrifying 'other' characters around her. Despite her fears, Coraline repeatedly pushes on. She encourages herself to keep going, seeks pragmatic solutions, and comforts herself in various ways, such as by whistling or singing. Some examples include the following.

- '"I'm not afraid," she told herself. "I'm not." She did not believe herself, but she scrambled on to the old stage …' (p.118)
- 'She had never been so scared, but still she walked forward until she reached the sac.' (p.119)
- 'She hugged herself, and told herself that she was brave, and she almost believed herself …' (p.133)
- 'She tried to whistle, but nothing happened, so she sang out loud instead, a song her father had made up for her …' (p.179)

Coraline's understanding of bravery – 'when you're scared but you still do it anyway' (p.72) – is heavily informed by an event that occurred when she was younger. Her father allowed himself to be badly stung by wasps in order to save her, then later returned to retrieve his glasses:

> And he said that wasn't brave ... standing there and being stung ... It wasn't brave because he wasn't scared: it was the only thing he could do. But going back again to get his glasses, when he knew the wasps were there, when he was really scared. *That* was brave. (p.71)

In addition, Coraline's defiance of the other mother, despite her fears, appears to have an impact on the other world – when she tells the other mother she is not afraid, the world seems to 'shimmer' (p.75), and as Coraline recovers the ghost souls, it begins deteriorating. Coraline's persistence in being brave, despite the great danger around her, defines her journey, and emphasises the importance of continuing on, rather than giving in to fear.

Love

Key quotes

'Still, the proudest spirit can be broken, with love.' (the other mother, p.92)

'It was true: the other mother loved her. But she loved Coraline as a miser loves money, or a dragon loves its gold. In the other mother's button eyes, Coraline knew that she was a possession, nothing more.' (p.124)

'And then a voice that sounded like her mother's – her own mother, her real, wonderful, maddening, infuriating, glorious mother, just said, "Well done, Coraline," and that was enough.
The door started to slip closed, easily as anything.' (pp.154–5)

Love is a significant theme in *Coraline*, and can be considered through the contrast between the other mother and Coraline's real family.

The other mother's love: manipulation and control

The other mother repeatedly claims to love Coraline, seeming to want to usurp the position of Coraline's real mother. To do this, she engages in highly manipulative tactics to try to force Coraline to stay and love her back. She makes herself resemble Coraline's real mother and creates the 'other' characters and the entire other world to entice Coraline to join her 'big happy family' (p.58). The world and the other mother's actions, as discussed in 'Growing up' (pp.47–9), seem to be trying to improve on aspects of Coraline's real world that were troublesome to her, such as her boredom and her real parents' lack of attention to her:

> 'Where are my parents?' Coraline asked.
> 'We're here,' said her other mother, in a voice so close to her real mother's that Coraline could scarcely tell them apart. 'We're here. We're ready to love you and play with you and feed you and make your life interesting.' (p.73)

However, the 'other' characters and the entire other world itself are revealed to be an illusion. Each of the 'other' characters is nothing more than a 'ghastly parody' (p.137); the world devolves into a 'formless, swirling mist' (p.122) and the other mother becomes visibly monstrous: 'huge', with hair that 'writhed and twined about her head' and teeth 'sharp as knives' (p.149). The ease with which the illusion falls apart reflects how false and insubstantial it truly was.

Along with the creation of the illusory other world, the other mother behaves in various manipulative ways towards Coraline throughout the story.

- She kidnaps Coraline's parents to force her back into the other world.
- She creates an illusion of Coraline's parents in a mirror to deceive her into thinking they don't want her anymore.
- She tries to make Coraline doubt others, calling the ghosts 'liars' (p.107) and the cat 'vermin' (p.147). Similarly, when Coraline notices the other mother isn't reflected in the mirror, the other mother says that mirrors 'are never to be trusted' (p.92).

→

- She gives Coraline the key to the flat with the dangerous other father in the cellar, under the pretext of helping her.
- She agrees to Coraline's game but does not follow through on her end of the bargain when Coraline wins, instead sending her hand to follow Coraline into the real world.

Despite the other mother's claims to love Coraline, she manipulates and lies to her from the very beginning. The use of manipulation is a form of control, and the other mother behaves in many other controlling ways throughout the novel. One significant way in which she does this is by relying on her false position as a 'mother'. To dismiss Coraline's concerns and rebellions against her, she uses language that adults might use towards misbehaving children, such as 'we only want what's best for you' (p.58) and 'this is for you, Coraline. For your own good. Because I love you' (p.95).

Key point

The other mother's assertion that 'the proudest spirit can be broken, with love' (p.92) is particularly unnerving, revealing the other mother's overall attitude towards love. Her love is not about Coraline, but about what she herself wants, and the role she wants Coraline to play in her fantasy of a happy family.

The revelation that the other mother fed on the ghost children until they had 'nothing left' (p.101), the cat's suggestion that 'it's hard to tell' if the other mother wants 'something to love' or 'something to eat' (p.79), and the description of the other mother looking at Coraline 'hungrily' (p.74) are similarly telling of the nature of the other mother's love – a love defined by a desire to possess to the point of consumption. For the other mother, love, possession and total control are intertwined, leading her to behave in a horrendous manner towards the objects of her affection.

Coraline's parents' love: strength and support

Despite Coraline's mother and father's inattentiveness at the beginning of the novel, Coraline and her parents' love for each other is founded on deep bonds of trust and care, and the power of this love is revealed as the story progresses.

In the second half of the book particularly, Coraline thinks of her parents and finds their love for her to be a significant source of support, even when they are not physically present. Her father's rescue of her from wasps when she was younger both demonstrates his deep love for her and shapes her understanding of bravery – a kind of bravery that she emulates to help her through her journey. She also sings a song he had made up for her, to help manage her fear. The lyrics – *'I give you lots of kisses, / And I give you lots of hugs'* (p.179) – demonstrate his affection, and the fact that Coraline thinks about his song when she feels afraid signals that she feels comforted by a memory of him. Her mother's love is similarly important for Coraline. Her mother's words of encouragement – 'Well done, Coraline' (p.155) – enable Coraline to shut the door against the other mother during the final escape from the other world.

Rather than seeking to control her, Coraline's parents provide her with the strength and support she needs to continue. In turn, Coraline's deep affection for her parents means that she doesn't hesitate to return to the dangerous other world to rescue them: 'I'm going back for them because they are my parents. And if they noticed I was gone I'm sure they would do the same for me' (p.72).

The extent to which Coraline is influenced by her parents' care for her demonstrates the power of familial love, suggesting that love can be a positive influence that one can draw on as a source of comfort and strength. In this way, this love is much more powerful than that of the other mother, who can offer only a warped imitation – like her creations – of what Coraline shares with her real parents.

Identity

Key quotes

'I asked you not to call me Caroline. It's Coraline.' (p.12)

'There was nothing reflected in it but a young girl in her dressing gown and slippers, who looked like she had recently been crying but whose eyes were real eyes, not black buttons …' (p.74)

'A husk you'll be, a wisp you'll be, and a thing no more than a dream on waking, or a memory of something forgotten.' (ghost child, p.102)

Identity is a key aspect of Coraline's journey. Her struggles with identity – feeling ignored by others, wishing for individuality, and needing to resist the other mother's attempts to consume her – are hinted at early on, with her 'drawing' of 'MIST' (p.26). Coraline writes the word with the 'I' on a line by itself:

M ST
I

As critic David Rudd notes, the 'I' can be considered a pronoun representing Coraline herself, and the drawing can have more than one interpretation. The placement of the 'I' separately from the other letters could represent Coraline feeling alone and ignored by those around her, possibly desiring the mist to 'descend and embrace, or envelope her' as the other mother later tries to do, or alternatively, it might represent Coraline's 'refus[al] to be contained' and her desire to hold on to her independence (Rudd 2008).

Later in the story, the other mother's desire to control and possess her means that Coraline must maintain a strong sense of self to avoid being consumed. One way she does this is by repeatedly resisting the other mother and asserting her independence, such as by rejecting the other mother ('I don't want your love … I don't want anything from you', p.124); changing into her own pyjamas rather than wearing clothes from the other world ('If I'm going to do this … I'm not going to do it in her clothes', p.115); and refusing to accept food from the other father ('I don't need a snack … I have an apple. See?', p.74).

The theme of identity is represented in different ways throughout the novel, including through the ghost children, the focus on names and the symbol of the button eyes.

The ghost children

When Coraline meets the ghost children, they have almost entirely lost their identities to the other mother and are faint and insubstantial. This absence of identity is presented through metaphors reiterating a sense of loss and insubstantiality: 'snakeskins and spiderhusks' (p.101) and 'a dream on waking, or a memory of something forgotten' (p.102).

The ghost children remember snapshots of moments from their lives, but they have difficulty remembering aspects of their identities such as their names:

> We keep our memories longer than our names. I still keep pictures in my mind of my governess on some May morning ... the morning sun behind her, and all the tulips bobbing in the breeze. (p.97)

When Coraline asks one of the ghost children if it is a boy or a girl, it appears uncertain, but works out that it is a boy by sifting through memories: 'they ... gave me britches and cut my hair' (p.99). Further, upon recalling this aspect of itself, the ghost 'glowed a little more brightly' (p.99), suggesting that the act of remembering themselves helps the ghosts become more substantial and indicating that memory is integral to identity. The importance of memory is also reflected by the colours of the souls. The first soul that Coraline recovers is 'the colour of a scarlet-and-orange tulip nodding in the May sun' (p.114) – a direct reference to the ghost child's memory of tulips. When Coraline recovers his soul, he becomes more confident with his memories – 'I certainly *was* a boy, now I do think on it' (p.114) – suggesting that Coraline's act of rescuing him has helped him to remember who he once was.

Coraline's dream of the ghost children, after escaping the other world, shows all three appearing much more vividly. The detail in their descriptions here contrasts with their faintness in the other world and suggests that, by releasing them from the other world, Coraline has helped them to recover their identities as well.

Names

The importance of names is a recurring idea in *Coraline*. Before Coraline visits the other world, she is frustrated by her neighbours incorrectly calling her 'Caroline': 'I asked you not to call me Caroline. It's Coraline' (p.12). Their repeated inability to pronounce her name suggests dismissal of her value as a person.

After Coraline traps the other mother's hand, Mr Bobo finally listens to her and says her name 'with wonderment and respect' (p.183). Significantly, Coraline only learns his name in this same chapter – previously, she pejoratively referred to him as the 'crazy old man' (e.g. p.12). This suggests that she had held him in disregard. The importance of names is emphasised here, as by learning each other's names they demonstrate a new level of respect for one another. Names are also shown to be significant to one's sense of identity through the ghost children, who lose their names after being taken by the other mother: 'The names are the first things to go' (p.97).

However, the cat offers a different perspective on names, telling Coraline that people have names 'because you don't know who you are' whereas cats 'know who we are, so we don't need names' (p.48). The notion of knowing 'who you are' is pertinent during Coraline's struggle against the other mother: to fight back against the other mother's desire to possess and control her, Coraline must develop a strong sense of herself and who she is, in a way that is not reliant on other people.

The button eyes

The button eyes are a powerful symbol in the novel, representing the other mother's complete control over another person. The other mother and each of her creations have black buttons in place of eyes, and she wants to replace Coraline's eyes with black buttons, in exchange for her staying in the other world. Although the other mother describes it as 'a little thing' (p.57), this is an enormous ask. By allowing the other mother to replace her eyes with buttons, Coraline would presumably lose her sight and be unable to interact with the world in the same way. Additionally, eyes are a highly expressive physical feature and have great significance for a person's individuality. They are thought to provide a glimpse into a person's emotions and internal world, giving rise to the idiom 'eyes are the window to the soul'. The button eyes would hinder Coraline's ability to express herself and the other mother's plan to replace Coraline's eyes with buttons represents her desire to steal Coraline's soul entirely.

Key point

Buttons also have associations with toys and dolls, which sometimes have buttons for eyes. This association emphasises the dark nature of the other mother's request – she wishes to have full control over Coraline, reducing her to the role of a doll.

When Coraline looks at her reflection in the mirror, she takes comfort from the fact that she has her real eyes: 'a young girl ... who looked like she had recently been crying but whose eyes were real eyes, not black buttons' (p.74). To give up her eyes would be to lose her identity to the other mother.

Good overcoming evil

Key quote

'Fairy tales are more than true: not because they tell us that dragons exist, but because they tell us that dragons can be beaten.' (GK Chesterton, epigraph)

A central theme of the novel is the notion that good will overcome evil. This is alluded to in the epigraph at the very start of the novel, paraphrased from the writer GK Chesterton. The quote positions *Coraline* in the tradition of fairy tales (for more, see 'Genre, structure & language') and speaks directly to the intentions of the book – *Coraline* is a story that tells us 'dragons can be beaten'. Gaiman has explicitly stated that this was one of his intentions in writing *Coraline*: 'What is important is to tell [children] that a bad thing can be beaten … When I went into *Coraline*, that was what I held onto' (CBC Arts 2009).

The notion of good overcoming evil is apparent throughout Coraline's battle against the other mother. Coraline is motivated by good intentions – she seeks to rescue her parents and the ghost children – and demonstrates positive qualities such as love, compassion, wisdom, determination and bravery. These qualities help her earn the affection and support of the characters around her, such as the ghost children and the cat, and her loving relationship with her family also ensures she feels supported.

Coraline also receives advice from the mice through Mr Bobo and is given warnings through the tea-leaf readings by Miss Spink and Miss Forcible. Even the mirrors, when they are not actively being manipulated by the other mother, provide revelations that help Coraline progress with her quest. This suggests that there are wider forces of 'good' at play that are on Coraline's side.

The other mother is the 'dragon' of the story. She has selfish, harmful intentions and is terrifyingly powerful – she can 'build whole worlds' and then 'tear them down every night' (p.138), create and control monstrous creatures, and steal both children and adults. Rather than earning the support of others as Coraline does, she is manipulative and forceful, and rules through fear and control: 'when she gets out of sorts, she takes it out on everybody else' (p.130).

The contrast between Coraline's and the other mother's approaches and motivations sets up a binary of good and evil. Coraline's victory over the other mother demonstrates that good motivations and positive qualities can triumph over even the most dangerous of monsters.

DIFFERENT INTERPRETATIONS

Different interpretations arise from different responses to a text. Over time, a text will evoke a wide range of responses from its readers, who may come from various social or cultural groups and live in very different places and historical periods. Responses by critics and reviewers can be published in newspapers, journals and books, both online and in print. They can also be expressed in discussions among readers in the media, classrooms, book groups and so on.

While there is no single correct reading or interpretation of a text, it is important to understand that an interpretation is more than a personal opinion – it is the justification of a point of view on the text. To present an interpretation of a text based on your point of view, you must use a logical argument and support it with relevant evidence from the text.

The critics' viewpoints

As an acclaimed children's novel that uses fantasy to grapple with significant issues, *Coraline* has received much attention from critics and academics. Academic studies often consider such elements of the story as its themes of identity and coming of age, and its associations with fairy tales and Gothic literature. For example, Karen Coats, a professor who specialises in children's and young adults' literature, examines *Coraline* alongside two other works by Gaiman with a focus on its genre as children's Gothic literature, arguing that such literature provides representation of the fears and internal struggles of growing up: 'giving concrete expression to abstract psychic processes, keeping dark fascinations and haunting fears where children can see them' (Coats 2008).

David Rudd, an emeritus professor of children's literature, takes a psychoanalytical approach and analyses *Coraline* with a focus on its uncanny (mysterious yet familiar) elements, arguing that '*Coraline* is centrally concerned with how one negotiates one's place in the world'. He concludes by suggesting Coraline must realise that, like the other mother, 'she is the one being overly demanding', needing to learn that she cannot keep requiring the attention of those around her (Rudd 2008). Richard Gooding, an associate professor with an interest in children's literature, also considers the uncanny, but with a focus on the technical and stylistic features of *Coraline* and how these reflect Coraline's development, as well as a consideration of how adults and children might interpret the story differently (Gooding 2008).

Danielle Russell, an associate professor of English, takes a different approach, examining how Mrs Jones and the other mother might represent different types of mothers and arguing that *Coraline* 'should be read as part of an invigorating debate about mothering and motherhood in the twenty-first century' (Russell 2012).

Outside of academia, there are many reviews and discussions of *Coraline*, as well as fan theories demonstrating different ideas about or interpretations of the book, graphic novel and film. These include the idea that after Coraline goes to the other world, she never actually returns to the real world (The Fangirl 2016), and the idea that the other world is an enormous, ancient rat-like beast that has trapped and feeds on the other mother (Coy 2021).

Two interpretations

Interpretation 1: Coraline's personal qualities, including her self-reliance, bravery and intelligence, are what enable her to succeed against the other mother.

Although Coraline shares a large, subdivided house with five adults, she is left to protect herself against the dangerous other mother alone, relying on her own abilities to survive the other world.

From the beginning of the novel, Coraline is shown to be highly independent and self-reliant. The adults around her pay her little attention – her parents are too busy working to play with her, and her neighbours are so preoccupied with themselves that they call her 'Caroline', despite Coraline's repeated corrections. Forced to entertain herself, Coraline spends her time exploring her surroundings alone. Even after she discovers the dangers of the other world and the other mother, she cannot trust the adults around her to help: when she tells Miss Spink, Miss Forcible and the police officer her parents are missing, Miss Spink and Miss Forcible ignore her and the officer assumes she is recounting a nightmare. Her parents themselves, kidnapped by the other mother, are unable to provide help, and after Coraline rescues them they have no recollection of the other world. Because of this persistent lack of support from the adults around her, Coraline has no choice but to rely on her own capabilities to defeat the other mother.

Significant factors in Coraline's struggle with the other mother are her commitment to independence and her refusal to comply with the other mother's wishes or to fall for the lures of the other world. Early on, Coraline demonstrates a strong sense of her own interests and dislikes, attempting to persuade her mother to buy her interesting clothes and refusing to eat her father's recipes. This strong understanding of what she wants serves her in the other world as she goes up against the other mother. Despite the appeals of the other world, the importance Coraline places on her own independence and her love for her real family prevent her from agreeing to the other mother's proposal that she stay in the other world. Coraline actively rejects attempts to control her, deciding not to wear clothes from the other world and rejecting the other father's offer of food, and she is never tempted to play the child in the other mother's fantasy of a 'happy family' (p.58). Because of this, she avoids the terrible fate of the ghost children, 'fed on' by the other mother until they had 'nothing left' of themselves (p.101).

Finally, Coraline's victory over the other mother depends on her determination, courage and cunning. Though she frequently feels afraid in the other world, she pushes past her fear, reminding herself that she is 'brave' (p.74) and an 'explorer' (p.87) to help her persevere in the face of terrifying and monstrous characters and a world deteriorating before her eyes. She is also highly intelligent, outsmarting the other mother and her creations. She thinks of a 'challenge', giving herself the opportunity to rescue her parents and the ghost children; blinds the other father in the cellar to aid her escape; tricks the other mother into opening the drawing-room door; and, finally, traps the other mother's hand in the well by pretending to have a picnic with her dolls. Throughout the story, she repeatedly uses her persistence, resolution and quick wit to save herself, and others, from difficult situations.

As the winged ghost child tells her, Coraline has the 'blessings' of 'good fortune and wisdom and courage' (p.167). Although she is unable to rely on those around her for assistance, her personal qualities – including her bravery and intelligence – mean that she can depend upon herself instead, which ultimately leads to her success against the terrifying and powerful other mother.

Interpretation 2: Coraline is only able to succeed against the other mother because of the support of those around her.

In the face of the terrible danger of the other mother, Coraline needs all the help she can get, and her success is ultimately due to the support she receives from various sources throughout her journey.

Even before Coraline meets the other mother, she is given warnings, help and advice about the other world. Mr Bobo, whom she refers to as 'the crazy old man upstairs' (e.g. p.25), sends her a message from the mice warning her away from the door; and Miss Spink and Miss Forcible warn her she is in danger after reading her tea-leaves, and give her the stone with a hole in it to help with 'bad things' (p.31). When the other mother's hand follows Coraline into the real world, information from the tea-leaves and the behaviour of the mice, passed on to Coraline by her neighbours, again indicate she is in danger. Despite her neighbours' ignorance of the other world and the other mother, they provide Coraline with significant help throughout the novel. The stone, in particular, turns out to be invaluable, enabling Coraline to find the ghost souls and keeping her clear-headed in the illusory other world.

Coraline also receives assistance from several unexpected characters. Although the cat initially indicates it does not think much of her, it provides useful advice and information: it tells her to keep her 'protection' (p.49), shows her that her parents are trapped in the other world, advises her to 'challenge' the other mother, and kills the rat holding the third ghost child's soul. The ghost children similarly provide useful advice and information. They warn Coraline of what will happen should she agree with the other mother, tell her to 'look through the stone' (p.103), lend her strength to close the door against the other mother and, finally, warn her about the other mother's hand. Even the other father helps Coraline, though accidentally at first: he lets slip that there is 'only one key' (p.77) and that the other mother created the world. When Coraline meets him in the cellar, he urges her to run from him and tries to resist the other mother's imperative as long as he can before attacking her. The assistance from these characters is significant as, had they not chosen to help Coraline, she likely would not have been able to progress further against the other mother.

Finally, Coraline's parents, though not present for much of her journey in the other world, support her in persisting despite the frightening dangers around her. Coraline's memory of her father rescuing her from wasps helps her to understand courage and persevere despite her fears. The sound of her mother's voice encouraging her – 'Well done, Coraline' (p.155) – enables her to close the door against the other mother, and Coraline sings her father's affectionate song from when she was a baby to comfort herself as she lures the other mother's hand to her picnic trap. Even when her parents are not immediately available to help her, Coraline's memories of her father and the sound of her mother's voice provide her with comfort and encouragement, which helps her in her struggles.

Coraline receives some form of support from most of the characters in the novel – even, in the case of the mice, characters she never meets. The combined efforts of those around her play an enormous role in helping her in her journey, and without them, she would never have been able to escape and defeat the terrible other mother.

QUESTIONS & ANSWERS

This section focuses on your own analytical writing on the text, and gives you strategies for producing high-quality responses in your coursework and exam essays.

Essay writing – an overview

An essay on a literary work is a formal and serious piece of writing that presents your point of view on the text, usually in response to a given topic. Your 'point of view' in an essay is your interpretation of the meaning of the text's language, structure, characters, situations and events, supported by detailed analysis of textual evidence.

Analyse – don't summarise

In your essays it is important to avoid simply summarising what happens in a text.

- A **summary** is a description or paraphrase (retelling in different words) of the characters and events. For example: 'Macbeth has a horrifying vision of a dagger dripping with blood before he goes to murder King Duncan.'
- An **analysis** is an explanation of the real meaning or significance that lies 'beneath' the text's words (and images, for a film). For example: 'Macbeth's vision of a bloody dagger shows how deeply uneasy he is about the violent act he is contemplating, and conveys his sense that supernatural forces are impelling him to act.'

A limited amount of summary is sometimes necessary to let your reader know which part of the text you wish to discuss. However, always keep this to a minimum and follow it immediately with your analysis of what this part of the text is really telling us.

Plan your essay

Carefully plan your essay so that you have a clear idea of what you are going to say. The plan ensures that your ideas flow logically, that your argument remains consistent and that you stay on topic. An essay plan should be a list of **brief dot points** covering no more than half a page.

- Include your central argument or main contention – a concise statement of your overall response to the topic.
- Write three or four dot points for each paragraph, indicating the main idea and evidence/examples from the text. Note that in your essay you will need to *expand* on these points and *analyse* the evidence.

Structure your essay

An essay is a complete, self-contained piece of writing. It has a clear beginning (the introduction), middle (several body paragraphs) and end (the last paragraph or conclusion). It must also have a central argument that runs throughout, linking each paragraph to form a coherent whole. See examples of introductions and conclusions in the 'Analysing a sample topic' and 'Sample answer' sections.

The introduction establishes your overall response to the topic. It includes your main contention and outlines the main evidence you will refer to in the course of the essay. Write your introduction *after* you have done a plan and *before* you write the rest of the essay.

The body paragraphs argue your case – they present evidence from the text and explain how this evidence supports your argument. Each body paragraph needs:

- a strong **topic sentence** (usually the first sentence) that states the main point being made in the paragraph
- **evidence** from the text, including some brief quotations
- **analysis** of the textual evidence, with **explanation** of its significance and how it supports your argument
- **links back to the topic** in one or more statements, usually towards the end of the paragraph.

Connect the body paragraphs so that your discussion flows smoothly. Use some linking words and phrases such as 'similarly' and 'on the other hand', though don't start every paragraph like this. Another strategy is to use a significant word from the last sentence of one paragraph in the first sentence of the next.

Use key terms from the topic – or synonyms for them – throughout, so the relevance of your discussion to the topic is always clear.

The conclusion ties everything together and finishes the essay. It includes strong statements that emphasise your central argument and provide a clear response to the topic.

Avoid simply restating the points made earlier in the essay – this will end on a very flat note and imply that you have run out of ideas and vocabulary. The conclusion should be a logical extension of what you have written, not just a repetition or summary of it. Writing an effective conclusion can be a challenge. Try using these tips.

- Start by linking back to the final sentence of the second-last paragraph, rather than leaping to your main contention straight away – this helps your writing to flow.
- Use synonyms and expressions with equivalent meanings to vary your vocabulary. This allows you to reinforce your line of argument without being repetitive.

When planning your essay, think of one or two broad statements or observations about the text's wider meaning. These should be related to the topic and your overall argument. Keep them for the conclusion, since they will give you something 'new' to say but still follow logically from your discussion. The introduction will be focused on the topic, but the conclusion can present a wider view of the text.

Essay topics

1. Coraline would never have fully appreciated what she already had in the real world without her ordeal with the other mother.
   Discuss.

2. 'Spiders' webs only have to be large enough to catch flies.'
   How does Gaiman use figurative language to develop character, setting and story in *Coraline*?

3. 'I'm an explorer …'
   How does *Coraline* examine the importance of the roles people play in life?

4. 'Fairy tales are more than true …'
   What is the role of fairy tales in *Coraline*?

5. 'Be wise. Be brave. Be tricky.'
   These are the most important qualities Coraline needs to defeat the other mother.
   Do you agree?

6. *Coraline* suggests that defiance is an integral part of growing up.
   To what extent do you agree?

7. 'It is astonishing just how much of what we are can be tied to the beds we wake up in in the morning, and it is astonishing how fragile that can be.'
   Coraline tells us that 'what we are' is inherently fragile.
   Discuss.

8. 'And then we'll all be together as one big happy family …'
   How does *Coraline* explore the role of family relationships?

9. How does Gaiman use structure to shape our understandings of *Coraline*?

10. 'You're too clever and too quiet for them to understand. They don't even get your name right.'
    In order to be happy with her life in the real world, Coraline must accept that those around her will never understand her.
    Do you agree?

Vocabulary for writing on *Coraline*

Autonomy: self-sufficiency, the freedom to choose one's own actions and be independent.

Bildungsroman: a story in which the protagonist's journey to maturity or enlightenment is central to the narrative.

Character archetype: a type of character that recurs across different stories.

Doppelganger: a person who appears very similar to another person. In literature and folklore, these 'doubles' are often evil or bad luck.

Epigraph: a quotation, phrase or other brief piece of text at the beginning of a novel, which can help set expectations of what a story will be about.

Fairy tales: stories with origins in folklore. They often contain magical or mythical elements such as fairies and monsters.

Figurative language: language used in a non-literal way by authors to help describe scenes and immerse the reader in the story (e.g. metaphor, simile, personification, onomatopoeia).

Foreshadowing: a literary device in which events or signs in the story hint at events to come.

Gothic literature: a genre characterised by gloomy, morbid and frightening elements.

Imagery: descriptive language that creates an image in the mind of the reader.

Intertextuality: references in one text to another text or texts.

Motif: a particular image or concept repeated to highlight a theme or develop an idea.

Novella: a story that is shorter than a typical novel, but longer than a short story.

Onomatopoeia: a word that resembles the sound associated with the thing it describes.

Parallel world: a type of alternative world in a story. In many stories, it reflects the main world but differs in some significant ways.

Parody: an imitation of something.

Personification: the attribution of human-like qualities to an item, animal, idea or other element.

Symbol: an object or other element used to represent an additional meaning.

Third-person limited: a type of narrative point of view in which there is an 'outside' narrator (not a character in the story), which stays close to the point of view of a particular character.

Uncanny: unnaturally strange, both familiar and unfamiliar at the same time, giving rise to feelings of uneasiness, horror, fear or dread.

Analysing a sample topic

'I'm an explorer …'

How does *Coraline* examine the importance of the roles people play in life?

This topic asks you to consider the ways in which *Coraline* portrays the different roles that people have in their lives. The roles we take on can include those we play in relationships with others (as parents, friends, neighbours, partners etc.), as well as the roles that help us define who we are (e.g. you may choose to describe yourself as a book lover or a musician).

You are being asked about what *Coraline* suggests about the importance of roles in general, not just what it means for the characters in the novel, so you will need to think about what kind of messages *Coraline* conveys about roles in relation to identity and relationships.

The topic asks you to consider *how* the novel examines the importance of roles, so make sure you consider how the novel communicates these messages. Evidence could include any elements from the text such as the use of language, the actions of particular characters, and significant moments or events in the narrative.

Your response will need to address the quote that is part of this topic. This particular quote is spoken or thought by Coraline and appears more than once in the novel – understanding this context will provide a strong foundation for you to use it as evidence. The quote signals that the connection between role-playing and identity is significant and should be examined in your response.

Sample introduction

> Neil Gaiman's *Coraline* suggests that roles can be highly significant in terms of the way we behave, treat others and understand ourselves. The other mother seeks to force Coraline to occupy a particular role, with disastrous consequences, suggesting that trying to force someone to perform a role in a particular way can affect them negatively. Additionally, both Coraline and the other mother expect other characters to fulfil certain roles and are displeased when they do not (or cannot) achieve this, emphasising the importance of accepting others for who they are. However, roles can also be useful, particularly when we can choose them ourselves, as demonstrated when Coraline takes on the role of 'explorer' to help her through her ordeal in the other world.

Body paragraph outline

Paragraph 1: Forcing others to perform roles they do not want can have significant negative consequences.

- The other mother attempts to create her ideal of a 'big happy family' (p.58), with herself, the other father and Coraline.
- The other mother behaves in a highly controlling, unpleasant manner, kidnapping Coraline's parents, locking her behind a mirror and proposing to replace her eyes with buttons.
- Her affection for Coraline is conditional on Coraline behaving in the obedient 'child' role: 'if you will be a good child who loves her

mother, be compliant and fair-spoken, you and I shall understand each other perfectly and we shall love each other perfectly as well' (p.106).

- These actions make Coraline miserable and fuel her desire to escape, demonstrating the harmful consequences and futility of trying to force someone into a role they do not want.

Paragraph 2: Unrealistic expectations of how others will fulfil certain roles can lead to unhappiness, suggesting the need for acceptance and understanding.

- The other father tries to play the role of father in the other mother's fantasy ('I shall demonstrate our tender hospitality to you, such that you will not even think about ever going back', p.85).
- He is unable to achieve this and, instead, accidentally provides Coraline with information about the other world. As punishment for this, he is locked in a cellar with 'nothing but dust and damp and forgetting' (p.130).
- Coraline wants her parents to perform their roles slightly differently. She asks her father, 'Why don't you play with me?' (p.27), resentful of her parents' preoccupation with their own tasks. She is also unhappy with her mother for not buying her the clothing she wants and for listening to the shop assistant rather than to her (pp.33–4).
- Affection between Coraline and her parents is restored once Coraline accepts them for who they are (pp.159–62).

Paragraph 3: We can choose particular roles for ourselves, and these roles can have significant impacts on how we feel and behave.

- Coraline actively chooses to embody certain roles and qualities to alter her perception of herself. She calls herself 'an explorer' (p.24) early in the novel, and daydreams about 'exploring the Arctic, or the Amazon rainforest' (p.81). This is a form of self-expression as well as play.
- While in the dangerous other world, she encourages herself onward by thinking of this self-identification: 'I'm an explorer ... And I need all the ways out of here that I can get' (p.87).

➔

- Coraline acts like a young child, playing 'picnic' with her dolls, temporarily taking on the role that the other mother had tried to force on her. This helps her trap the hand in the well, demonstrating that roles can be strategically performed to achieve a particular aim.
- The ghost children did not choose their own roles, but instead played the role that the other mother wanted of them. This resulted in them having their identities taken from them, becoming 'hollow' (p.102), like 'snakeskins and spiderhusks' (p.101), suggesting that it is vital that we are free to choose our roles for ourselves.

Sample conclusion

In *Coraline*, the other mother and Coraline both aim to make use of or enforce various roles, each with significant impacts, but with greatly different outcomes. The effects of the other mother's controlling actions suggest that trying to force others to perform roles against their wishes can have deeply negative consequences. Conversely, Coraline's success in defeating the other mother indicates that roles and role-playing can be useful, and even a source of strength and resilience, when people are able to determine these roles for themselves.

SAMPLE ANSWER

'You're too clever and too quiet for them to understand. They don't even get your name right.'
In order to be happy with her life in the real world, Coraline must accept that those around her will never understand her.
Do you agree?

The other world in Neil Gaiman's *Coraline* appears to offer Coraline many things she wants, but can't have, in the real world. As the quote suggests, being understood is one such element. However, as she discovers, being happy is not about having whatever she wants. It is more important for Coraline to have autonomy and a strong understanding of herself than to rely on the perceptions of those around her.

Feeling understood is shown to be greatly important to Coraline early in the novel. She is surrounded by adults who ignore or dismiss her, and her first encounters with her neighbours show her irritably correcting their persistent mispronunciations of her name: 'I asked you not to call me Caroline. It's Coraline.' More than this, the adults' inability or refusal to listen to her has significant consequences later, forcing Coraline to confront the dangerous other mother alone. Miss Spink and Miss Forcible don't notice when Coraline tells them her parents are 'missing', and the police officer assumes she has had a nightmare when she asks for help. It seems likely that, after Coraline returns from the other world, she will continue to be dismissed and ignored, even to the point where she might need to deal with dangerous situations by herself.

However, as Coraline discovers, those in the other world do not understand her either, even if they appear to listen to her and say her name correctly. They offer her numerous things they think she wants and lacks in the real world: attention, nice food, nice clothes and entertainment. Yet these things don't make Coraline happy. She says to the other old man, 'What kind of fun would it be if I just got everything I ever wanted … and it didn't *mean* anything.' His confusion ('I don't understand'), demonstrates that he doesn't truly know her either – he and the other mother simply have a superficial knowledge of her likes and dislikes.

What's more important for Coraline is to learn that she doesn't need to rely on others, but instead should value her own strength and understanding of herself. One important moment in the narrative is when the cat tells her 'cats don't have names' because, unlike humans, 'we know who we are, so we don't need names'. This dismissal of names suggests that it is more important to have a strong sense of identity than to rely on others for validation. Significantly, the other mother tries to prevent Coraline from having her own sense of self, or any autonomy. She seeks to consume Coraline's identity entirely, as represented by the button eyes. The button eyes, associated with the artificial eyes of toys, are a visual marker of the other mother's ownership and control, and would prevent Coraline from being able to express herself or navigate the world as she had before. The other mother also tells Coraline that they will 'understand each other perfectly' only if Coraline behaves exactly as she wants her to, and is 'a good child who loves her mother ... compliant and fair-spoken'; by using phrases reminiscent of the kind used by parents, the other mother attempts to manipulate Coraline into accepting an extreme level of control. Consequently, Coraline must recognise the importance of her identity and freedom to maintain her autonomy, instead of focusing on whether others understand her.

Although the other old man's claim that people don't 'understand' Coraline holds some truth, what is much more important in facilitating Coraline's happiness is for her to protect her own understanding of who she is, which allows her to maintain her independence and seek meaning for herself. In fact, the conclusion of the novel suggests that, once Coraline can do this and let go of her expectations of others, she is more open to having a better understanding of them. When she finally addresses Mr Bobo by his name, he learns hers too, indicating that, if she does want others to 'understand' her, Coraline needs to be in a position where she can better understand and accept those around her first.

REFERENCES & READING

Text

Gaiman, N 2003, *Coraline*, Bloomsbury Publishing Plc, London.

Other resources

CBC Arts 2009, 'No real controversy over scary kids tale *Coraline*, author Gaiman says', CBC News, 5 February, https://www.cbc.ca/news/entertainment/no-real-controversy-over-scary-kids-tale-coraline-author-gaiman-says-1.837203

Coats, K 2008, 'Between horror, humour, and hope: Neil Gaiman and the psychic work of the Gothic', in A Jackson, K Coats & R McGillis (eds), *The Gothic in Children's Literature: Haunting the Borders*, Routledge, Abingdon & New York, pp.77–92.

Coy, M 2021, 'This twisted theory makes *Coraline* even darker than you remember', *Game Rant*, 16 April, https://gamerant.com/coraline-theory-darker-remember

Gaiman, N 2013, 'Introduction', *Coraline*, 10th anniversary edition, Bloomsbury Publishing Plc, London.

——2016, *The View from the Cheap Seats: Selected Non-fiction*, Headline Publishing Group, London.

Gooding, R 2008, '"Something very old and very slow": *Coraline*, uncanniness, and narrative form', *Children's Literature Association Quarterly*, Johns Hopkins University Press, vol. 22, no. 4, pp.390–407.

HarperCollins Publishers 2011, 'Neil Gaiman on the Origins of *Coraline*', 30 September, https://www.youtube.com/watch?v=sd4w6l9F--k

——2012, 'A *Coraline* Q&A with Neil Gaiman', Shelf Stuff, https://web.archive.org/web/20220720160238/https://www.shelfstuff.com/blog/a-coraline-qa-with-neil-gaiman

——2024, 'Meet Neil Gaiman', *Mouse Circus*, https://www.mousecircus.com/about

Lessons from the ScreenPlay 2020, 'How Coraline Borrows from Ancient Forms of Storytelling', 23 October, https://www.youtube.com/watch?v=NR3Q3IAMVXM

Olson, R 2002, 'The Booklist Interview: Neil Gaiman', *Booklist Magazine*, August, https://web.archive.org/web/20020912045005/http://www.ala.org/booklist/v98/aug/69interview.html

Rudd, D 2008, 'An eye for an I: Neil Gaiman's *Coraline* and questions of identity', *Children's Literature in Education*, vol. 39, pp.159–68.

Russell, D 2012, 'Unmasking m(other)hood: third-wave mothering in Gaiman's *Coraline* and *MirrorMask*', in T Prescott & A Drucker (eds), *Feminism in the Worlds of Neil Gaiman: Essays on the Comics, Poetry and Prose*, McFarland & Company, Inc., North Carolina, pp.161–76.

Rutherford, E 2014, 'Faerie Rules in the World of Coraline', Black Button Eyes Productions, 29 July, https://www.blackbuttoneyes.com/blog/2020/8/22/faerie-rules-in-the-world-of-coraline

StoryDive 2020, 'The Creepy, Real Myths & Lore Behind Coraline Explained! (Coraline Theory / Analysis)' 23 December, https://www.youtube.com/watch?v=fLpqKk0zu8A

The Fangirl 2016, '*Coraline* Book vs Movie Analysis and Theories – The Fangirl', 11 October, https://www.youtube.com/watch?v=6ScTFfjyWWc&t=1s